Long After Tonight is All Over

Pete McKenna

NEW HAVEN PUBLISHING LTD

Published 2024
First Edition
New Haven Publishing
www.newhavenpublishingltd.com
newhavenpublishing@gmail.com

Cover art © Howard Priestley – artist and author of:
Love Factory: The History of Holland Dozier Holland
Art and Soul
Soul Man: Deep in the Heart of America Lies its Soul

Cover Design © Pete Cunliffe

new haven

A POEM DEDICATED TO THE 100 CLUB OXFORD
STREET SOHO LONDON BY PAUL DAVIS – IRISH
AUTHOR – ACTOR – DEEJAY – LIFELONG MOD AND
NORTHERN SOULER

NORTHERN SOUNDS ON SOUTHERN STREETS
WEST END BOUND TO BASEMENT BEATS
AND LONG FORGOTTEN HEROES SOUNDS
IN THIS HEAVEN UNDERGROUND

WHERE SWEAT AND CONDENSATIONS MINGLE
WITH EVERY BEAT ANOTHER TINGLE
LEGENDS COVER WALLS AROUND
IN THIS HEAVEN UNDERGROUND

WE HEAR THE LOVE AND HEARTACHES TOO
OF THOSE WHO FAILED AND NEVER KNEW
THAT IS THIS PLACE IN LONDON TOWN
IN THE HEAVEN UNDERGROUND

WE LISTEN AND SING SONGS OF PRAISE
TO LONG FORGOTTEN DETROIT DAYS
THIS IS OUR WORLD WE ARE AT ITS HUB
THE LEGENDARY 100 CLUB

INTRODUCTION

The 23rd of September 2023 marked a monumental milestone in the history of alternative British club culture, celebrating what would have been the 50th anniversary of what many still claim to be the greatest northern soul venue ever: Wigan Casino Soul Club, a dilapidated Victorian former ballroom originally called The Empress, situated in a grimy central Lancashire town steeped in the faded heritage of the Industrial Revolution.

During the 60s and 70s, ballrooms across the country fell into decay, unable to compete with the new discotheques. The old ballroom occupied what was seen as valuable land going to waste, so plans to demolish it were being talked over when a young guy called Russ Winstanley somehow convinced the town council to let him lease the ballroom with the intention of opening a nightclub - and that's exactly what Russ managed to do. On Saturday 23rd September 1973 it was a hesitant Russ who opened for business, unsure as to whether the club would be a success or a total failure. That night some six hundred soul fans came to dance the night away, and the rest, as they say, is history.

As soon as the word got round about this all-nighter in an old ballroom in Wigan, the Casino quickly became the weekend home for all of us who were into northern soul. It was filled with people from all over the country, soaked in amphetamine sweat. In 1981, following Wigan Town Council's decision not to renew the club's all-night licence, Wigan Casino was burnt to the ground following a mysterious fire. The unanswered question, hanging in the air, was who or what caused the fire. My mates and I were truly gutted, hearing that our weekend home from home was gone forever, joining a lot of people who'd made the effort to travel to Wigan to see for themselves the final burning embers of Wigan Casino. Six years of my life flickered away before my eyes. To me, Wigan burning down was a right and fitting end to the place we'd all spent countless unforgettable hours in. RIP WIGAN CASINO SOUL CLUB SEPTEMBER 1973 – DECEMBER 1981. GONE BUT NEVER FORGOTTEN. The memory of it is commemorated with a simple plaque in the town centre.

Shortly after moving to Spain a few years back, I was giving my work space a long overdue spring clean, getting rid of a mass of old paperwork and countless unfinished manuscripts, when I came across the reviews I had forgotten all about following the publication of my first book, *Nightshift*, which recalled my good, bad and ugly memories of my six years as a member of Wigan Casino Soul Club, with vivid reality tinged with occasional regret.

The reviews took me back to far happier times in my life, living in Brighton for most of the 1990s in a cosy, one-bedroomed ground floor Georgian apartment overlooking the sea, working with a bunch of stonemasons who were building a hotel and office complex in the centre of town. Life was good: it was a time of optimism and ambition, with some of my dreams for a better future intact. I settled down to write *Nightshift* on a primitive but effective Sharp word processor which took me ages to get my head round. Writing and finishing the book were two things I accomplished, but finding a publisher and an agent proved an extremely difficult mountain to climb, going through the pages of the latest *Writers and Artists Yearbook* with no success.

At the very moment I was about to throw in the towel and move on to something else to waste all my spare time on - bingo! A small but respectable publisher called George Marshall, who wrote the acclaimed skinhead bible *Spirit Of 69* and owned St Publishing, contacted me with the good news that he was going through my story with a view to publishing it. Several weeks later I had a phone call from George Marshall telling me how well the book was selling, and not only selling but also pulling in some complimentary acclaim from many people in the know. I was over the moon and quickly sat down to write a follow up to *Nightshift* called *Who The Hell's Frank Wilson*. It was a dark, gritty, stylish, violent fictional story featuring a retired gangster with a passion for soul music called Ronnie Hardman, who goes on the warpath after discovering that his number one favourite soul record has been stolen - and God help those responsible when Ronnie gets his hands on them because they will be dead for sure. Once again, as was the case with *Nightshift*, *Who The Hell's Frank Wilson* pulled in some great reviews.

In the midst of my mega clean up, I found an old unfinished manuscript written in terrible, almost illegible long hand thanks to too many malt whiskies before hitting the sack after the end of another thankless day on the building site. The pages had yellowed, a stark reminder of just how fast time slips by on a journey we all face, summed up perfectly by Paul Weller who once wrote "blink and you just might miss it." With it almost completed, I thought: why the hell not get it done, putting other projects on hold to finish my trilogy on the northern soul scene before moving into uncharted waters.

Since *Nightshift* became available, there have been a multitude of books recalling various different aspects of the northern soul scene as we know it, so the pressure was on for me to find an angle, something different, dare I say unique, to help my story stand out from the rest - but what? What I didn't want to write was another all dancing, backdropping, spinning, clapping, singing, handshaking and hugging amphetamine-fuelled affair. Of course, there had to be a strong element of all that, but I didn't want that to be the main driving force behind the story.

I wanted to take the reader on more of a factual journey through the northern soul scene, from its early roots in 1960s London to the present day massive three-day northern soul extravaganzas taking place in the Victorian splendour of the Winter Gardens in Blackpool, the town where I was born and lived for many years. In between finishing off my story, my attention was drawn to the television programme celebrating the eightieth anniversary of Operation Overlord, the codename for the Normandy landings that took place on the 6th of June 1944, following a whole year of secretive, meticulous planning in assembling the greatest sea borne invasion force in military history, under the strict orders of the supreme Allied commander and US President Dwight Eisenhower. The plan was to land on five beaches, named as Gold, Juno, Sword, Utah and Omaha. The force consisted of one hundred and fifty-six thousand Allied troops from different nations, backed up by five thousand battleships and destroyers with eleven thousand fighters and bombers acting as air support for the troops on the beaches. The weather was atrocious, so much so that on the 5th of June, Eisenhower called off the original invasion time; but he was determined that there would be no more waiting around, so upon his orders the armada set off for the Normandy coastline, with all those involved knowing full well that the war was going to be won or lost in the next twenty-four hours.

Prior to the Normandy Landings, many of the Senate's powerful politicians were totally against sending their troops in to fight what many thought was a lost cause. One of the reasons for this was the fact that America had lost over one hundred and sixteen thousand soldiers in the trenches in the First World War, and they did not want to see that happening again - and in some ways who could blame them for not wanting to get involved in yet another costly war thousands of miles away from home? On the other hand, President Roosevelt felt honour-bound to assist his friend Winston Churchill and the beleaguered British nation in their hour of need. The US ambassador at the time, Joseph Kennedy, was dead against helping Britain, openly advising the Senate not to give any assistance to Britain and saying that for them it was only a matter of time before Hitler's forces invaded Britain. In addition, Kennedy chose to walk down a treacherous path by trying his best to arrange a meeting with Adolf Hitler to guarantee to the Fuhrer face to face that there would not be the slightest American involvement in the war, because in his opinion, Britain was dead and buried.

When news of this dreadful treachery reached Teddy Roosevelt, he promptly replaced Kennedy with Bill Donovan, who was fully convinced that Britain would stand firm against the Nazi onslaught and that America should support Britain with every means at America's disposal, calling to send arms, fuel and anything else Britain needed to keep fighting. With an election looming, things didn't look too good for President Roosevelt, who was seen as a war monger by many in the Senate, which could so easily have seen him kicked out of the White House; but luck prevailed despite a strong public outcry, and he was once again sworn in as President of the United States. He got straight to work to supply Britain with everything it needed, as fast as possible, running the gauntlet of the German submarine packs that took a huge toll on the American supply ships both in materials and lives lost. Churchill later claimed in his war diaries that whoever won that battle would go on to win the war - and he was proved correct. By the time Hitler had given up fighting Britain, he turned his attention to invading Russia, a decision that eventually cost him the war, fighting on two fronts - something most of his generals had advised him against.

Then on the 7th December 1941, America had no choice but to enter the war when the Japanese attacked Pearl Harbor, seriously damaging eight battleships and one hundred and eighty aircraft and killing over two thousand personnel, with over a thousand badly wounded. It was a cold, calculating act of aggression from Japan, which would see the country brought to its knees when America dropped two atom bombs on Hiroshima and Nagasaki four years later, an act which changed the shape of warfare forever. With the war raging in the Pacific, America still managed to flood Britain with thousands of troops and tons of equipment to prepare for the invasion of Normandy. As soon as the naval fleet anchored up, they began relentlessly pounding the German defences while the soldiers clambered down rope ladders and into the waiting landing craft, where they were packed in like sardines, tossed up and down and side to side, ashen faced, many of them vomiting, trying to keep their fears under control, each praying to their own gods to get them through the day in one piece, wondering if they were going to see their families, loved ones and friends ever again on one of the greatest days in European history. If successful, it would be the beginning of the end for Nazi Germany.

Surprisingly, the Allied landings on Gold, Sword, Juno and Utah beaches were met with little or no resistance, but on Omaha beach, the American soldiers had most definitely drawn the short straw. From the second the landing craft doors dropped open, the US soldiers were met with a withering, incessant, glowing hot storm of machine gun bullets, artillery shells and mortars from the German defences on top of the cliffs. That unforgettable, terrible opening scene in *Saving Private Ryan* when the first soldier off the landing craft gets killed by a bullet through his steel helmet gave us a very real, chilling insight into what those young US soldiers faced, trapped in the blood-red waters, death and screams of the terrified, wounded and dying as all hell exploded around them, struggling in vain to get to the cliffs where they could at least find some semblance of cover to allow them to catch their breath and regroup. In the end it was down to the sheer bravery and determination of the American Rangers, who carried out nigh on impossible orders to scale the cliffs by rope and take out the German defenders so the troops below could begin the advance away from the beach head and on to firmer ground inland.

I was glued to the screen for the memorial celebration: I found it to be a very humble, moving experience, especially seeing the old veterans who were once young men, now in the very late autumn of their lives, many unable to walk, wheelchair-bound but yet there they were, having made the arduous journey to be reunited with their friends and colleagues for the final time, the memory of whom they have kept inside them forever, along with the names of the places they fought in. Tears were streaming down their faces as they read the names on the gravestones in the neatly manicured cemeteries, helped by young soldiers, remembering a certain look, a glint in the eye and a smile from the faces piling into the landing craft before they hit the beach and began the long bloody road to Berlin.

On a day when the Allied commanders fully expected the casualties to be extremely high, the price paid for achieving such a monumental victory on that day was this: out of a total of one hundred and thirty-two thousand, seven hundred and fifteen British, Canadian and American soldiers who stormed the beaches that day, three thousand four hundred were killed or missing in action, in addition to which some twenty thousand Allied paratroopers suffered the same fate, fighting for the freedom many of us take for granted.

Fast forward to the wars in Iraq and Afghanistan and once again British and American soldiers were fighting and dying together in wars that many say should never have happened, as the fruitless search for Saddam Hussein's mythical weapons of mass destruction began in earnest, with him ending up on the gallows after being sentenced to death. These were wars in which the improvised explosive device really came into its own as a simple but deadly effective weapon, killing and maiming thousands of soldiers. The Iraq and Afghanistan wars cost the lives of seven thousand and ninety-four British and American soldiers, leaving thousands more injured.

Thankfully our longstanding alliance with America doesn't only apply to times of war. Our two countries share another, equally strong unbreakable alliance, and that is our deep love of music, stretching back to the early blues and jazz scene in the thirties and forties, when artists from both countries took the trouble to come and play in front of British and American audiences. As far as this story goes, though, there is one music genre in particular that has captured our passion and imagination for decades, and that is rare, imported, early American rhythm and blues music from the 1950s through to the 1960s, which went on to be christened northern soul. It's a music scene still very much into that early music which is just as popular today - if not more so - than it was back then in swinging 60s London, where it was initially played to enthusiastic audiences digging the new sounds in the four main mod clubs, these being the 100 Club, the Flamingo Club, the Scene Club, and the Bag O' Nails club, which were hugely influential in making sure this cool, new, fresh underground scene was here to stay. Ladies and gentlemen, I give you northern soul, simply put a music produced in America that is still championed in the United Kingdom some sixty years after it was introduced. As such this story is wholeheartedly dedicated to everyone who has contributed their bit in making the northern soul scene such a magical, discerning, genuinely alternative scene to be a part of, from shop and club owners to artists, record producers, promoters, collectors, deejays and, of course, the dancers. This is for you lot. LOL Pete McKenna.

ONE

1945 saw Britain gripped in the immediate financial and social aftermath of winning the war, which included the enormous debt owed to America for its timely intervention in our hour of need. With the country's gold reserves at a dangerous all time low, Britain appeared to be close to bankruptcy, and a thick cloud of seemingly endless austerity blanketed the country for many years. Restaurants were strictly limited to serving meagre portions, limited to three courses per person, and essential food items were rationed up until 1954, forcing the country's housewives to be more cost effective when cooking the family meals. The general public could be forgiven for thinking that the newly elected Labour government under Clement Attlee was doing nothing to tackle the crisis, but oh how wrong they would have been. Attlee was forced to make a series of tough decisions for the benefit of the country which he knew full well that the Tories would both hate and oppose. He took the unprecedented, audacious move of nationalising the centuries-old financial centre, the Bank of England, for the first time in its history. Railways, coal, iron and steel were also nationalised to maximise the profit away from the wealthy money-grabbing bosses into the country's coffers. Attlee also sold off many countries that were once part of the British Empire back to their rightful owners, as well as selling many military bases.

Working tirelessly alongside Attlee was the brilliant deputy Labour leader Aneurin Bevan, dedicated socialist, concerned philanthropist and vehement Tory hater. He came from a very humble background, born in the Welsh mining town of Tredegar, in which ninety percent of the inhabitants relied on mining to give them a living. Indeed, Aneurin worked in the pits himself, as well as being a butcher's boy, so he understood all about hard work before he responded to the call to take up politics. The housing crisis in the country was indeed a gigantic problem, with over seven hundred thousand homes in London alone needing repairing, as well as many outdated slums across the country. In the four years following the war, Aneurin was responsible for the building of eight hundred and fifty thousand homes, and his one big dream was to create a more traditional, social way of life, which he described as follows: "We should try to introduce in our modern villages and towns…where the doctor, the grocer, the butcher and the farm labourer all lived in the same street. I believe that is essential for the full life of the citizen…to see the living tapestry of a mixed community."

During a Labour party rally in 1948 he summed up his everlasting hatred of the Tories in the following words. "No amount of cajolery and no attempts at ethical or social seduction can eradicate from my heart a deep burning hatred for the Tory party… So far as I am concerned they are lower than vermin." Aneurin Bevan's greatest lasting legacy to the nation was the creation of the National Health Service, promising free medical and dental treatment for all, be they young or old. Mister Aneurin Bevan, a true crusading socialist rebel without a pause.

The 1957 general election saw the return of the Conservative Party under the new leadership of Harold Macmillan. That same year he shook the Houses of Parliament to their very core by announcing his plan to abolish conscription. This eventually came into force in 1960. For the very first time in our country's illustrious history, British youth were no longer ordered to march off to foreign lands they couldn't even spell to risk injury and death for King or Queen. Nobody could have envisaged that such a move would open the floodgates to a nationwide succession of home grown street cultures, many of which are still thriving today. Greasers, rockers, bikers, skinheads, suedeheads, boneheads, goths, ravers, casuals, psychobillies, rockabillies, mods and soulies - if you happen to be a past or present serving member of any of the above, don't ever ask the question 'What have the Tories ever done for us?' Living through the 1950s had been a tough ordeal for so many people, as families across the country huddled around their televisions and radios and crowds of well wishers packed Trafalgar Square for the countdown, hoping and praying that things were going to get better for everybody. "5 - 4 - 3 - 2 - 1 - Happy New Year everybody! Welcome to the 1960s" - and how.

The 1960s heralded a massive nationwide economic boom, in which jobs and money were plentiful, as the popular song 'England Swings Like A Pendulum' told its own story. Employment was booming, with people being able to afford luxury items like fridges, ovens, televisions and motor cars. The acclaimed designer Terence Conran opened his store Habitat in Chelsea, giving people the chance to furnish their homes with the very latest affordable designer furniture. The aircraft industry gave us the Vickers VC10, the BAC One Eleven and the most beautiful futuristic aircraft of all time, Concorde, offering its wealthy passengers the thrills of flying from London to New York in just three and a half hours at twice the speed of sound. Tragically Concorde crashed on the 25th July 2000 carrying a full load of fuel and passengers, who were all killed. It was a freak accident: the engine sucked in a small piece of sharp metal lying on the runway, causing it to explode, along with the glamour and excitement of supersonic commercial aviation that was Concorde.

The UK motoring industry was on a high, giving us one of the most iconic cars of the 60s, the Mark Two Jaguar saloon, with its distinctive leaping cat bonnet mascot, sumptuous leather hide and polished burr walnut interior, chrome wire wheels and a choice of engine size, and all for around fifteen hundred pounds. There then followed what Enzo Ferrari himself called the prettiest car ever built. The stunning Jaguar E-Type was unveiled at the Geneva motor show in 1961 and became an instant worldwide success for its beauty and performance for two thousand one hundred and sixty pounds, which was less than the cost of the Ferrari 250GT. And then there was the Mini, which for many people became the ultimate 60s iconic motoring statement and starred in one of the best British films at the time, *The Italian Job*. It was the brainchild of British Greek designer Sir Alex Issigonis who, apart from the classic Mini, created other variants such as the Traveller, the Moke, the Countryman, the Pick Up and the Van and the mighty Mini Cooper and Cooper S. The latter boasted a 1275cc engine that was powerful enough to have claimed three victories in the Monte Carlo Rallies of 1964, 1965 and 1967, driven by ace rally driver Belfast-born Paddy Hopkins and his wing man Henry Liddon.

And then of course there was that other iconic mini and one of an entirely different design to that of Alex Issigonis, which created equal amounts of disgust and approval after making its debut on the streets of London. The famous mini skirt that took the world by storm was designed by the then queen of fashion Mary Quant, who was based on the Kings Road in a shop she called Bazaar, and modelled by Jean Shrimpton and Twiggy, another great 60s icon with her own distinct look. Carnaby Street quickly became the epicentre of the new fashion industry, with John Stephens opening up five shops on the street which all became *the* places to shop for the army of fashionable teenagers who were looking for something that bit different to keep them ahead of the rest. One shop owner called Irvine Sellers, who was the man behind the Tom Cat Boutique, pulled off a truly remarkable publicity stunt by having Tom Jones walk up and down Carnaby Street arm in arm with the *Casino Royale* actress Christine Cooper with a cheetah on a lead. We even won the World Cup with a win over the old foe on that glorious Wembley afternoon - which won't happen again in my lifetime - and Manchester United beat Benfica to with the European Cup with a scintillating solo goal from the mercurial George Best.

With conscription abolished, British youth enjoyed a freedom denied to previous generations which saw the mods arriving on the scene with their sharp tailored suits, customised Italian scooters and pockets full of spare cash to burn dancing the night away high on drynamil - speed - mod food - in trendy London clubs like The Flamingo and The Scene to commercial American soul music. Despite the big three Stateside record labels - Stax, Atlantic and Tamla Motown - working flat out in a bid to feed the increasing appetites of British soul fans, the demand far outweighed supply. To remedy the situation a constellation of smaller satellite record labels across America began producing a continuous supply of rhythm and blues music for the discerning mods, but as the old saying goes, good things never last forever; or at least for the mods they didn't. Shortly after that infamous bank holiday in 1964 when mods clashed with rockers, fighting pitched battles in Brighton, the fate of the original mod scene was sealed. A fair number of diehard mods remained true to their beliefs of living life with a modicum of decency but many of them joined the new acid-dropping hippy scene, turning on, tuning in and dropping out, swapping their sharp haircuts and suits for long hair, beards, beads, loons and rainbow coloured paisley shirts.

A much darker incident took place in the 1960s between July 1963 and October 1965 when a series of brutal sadistic child murders shocked the nation. Five children - Keith Bennett, Pauline Reade, John Kilbride, Edward Evans and Leslie Ann Downey - were kidnapped and subjected to unimaginable torture and sexual abuse before they were killed and buried on Saddleworth Moor, a dark and foreboding place indeed. The killers were Ian Brady and Myra Hindley, who lived at number sixteen Warble Brock

Avenue in Hattersley, Lancashire. The two of them even tape recorded the screams of the children for their own sick, twisted, depraved self gratification, which later saw a number of tough, seasoned detectives brought to tears after listening to the tape.

Ian Brady, from Scotland, was an intelligent, well-read, egotistical man who greatly admired Adolf Hitler and demanded that those around him did as he told them and paid him the respect he thought he deserved for allowing them to spend time with him. Underneath all this intelligent charade beat the cold blooded heart of a truly sadistic psychopath. As for Myra Hindley, many people spoke about her as a normal, popular, down-to-earth girl who liked going out with her friends at the weekend; but that was before Myra met Ian. She quickly fell under his strong hypnotic spell. Whenever he told her to do something for him she would automatically obey without question. Myra dyed her hair blonde and started dressing differently to please Ian, short skirts, tight low-cut dresses, high-heeled shoes and boots giving her a much more provocative image, which the press picked up on with that truly sinister photograph of her staring coldly into the camera with thick make up and bleached blonde hair.

Sentencing the pair to life imprisonment, Judge Fenton Atkins summed them up as follows: "two sadistic killers of the utmost depravity." Perhaps for his own safety, Brady asked to be kept in solitary confinement for his entire sentence. Myra, who at first denied all knowledge of the murders, later confessed by admitting "my crime was worse than Brady's because I enticed the children as they would never have entered the car without my role." The one remaining child buried on Saddleworth Moor was Keith Bennett, whose family pleaded with Brady to show them where he was buried so he could have a proper funeral. Brady played a truly evil cat and mouse game with the family, sometimes agreeing and disagreeing at whim to help them locate their son, and I'm sure he enjoyed every second of their pain and anguish, spending hundreds of hours searching the moors to no avail. Meanwhile Myra showed genuine remorse for her part in the murders, turning to God to give her absolution and attracting the attentions of the fruitcake Conservative Lord Longford, who campaigned long and hard to get Myra released on the grounds that she should be given the second chance he thought she so richly deserved. The two of them became close; many people said too close, as Longford became more and more obsessed with Myra, who in my opinion was safer left in jail, where she eventually died.

One idyllic Sunday afternoon my dad took my mum and me for a drive in the countryside, stopping off at a pub which a good friend of his owned when my dad was a detective, back in the day. A dapper man in a smart three piece suit, shirt and tie, with slicked-back hair, he looked well pleased to see my dad after such a long time. His name was Albert Pierrepoint; quite an unusual name, I thought; but so was his profession, being the official state executioner, following in his father's and uncle's footsteps - that put a whole surreal meaning to the old phrase 'like father, like son'. In a long career, the exact number of people Albert hanged is uncertain: some say it was just over four hundred, while others claim it was over six hundred. After the war he was called in to hang the Nazi commandant of Belsen, along with many members of his staff, executed two at a time, after which he travelled up to Nuremberg, having been given the task of hanging the high-ranking Nazis found guilty of war crimes.

Throughout his career, Albert was proud of the fact that he went about his job with the utmost professionalism, treating those before him with a certain amount of respect no matter what crime they had committed. After a long career, Albert suddenly had a change of heart, becoming a main figure supporting the abolition of capital punishment.

18

In his autobiography, which makes very interesting reading, he said of hanging: "Hanging is said to be a deterrent. I cannot agree. There have been murders since the beginning of time. It is I who faced them last, young lads and girls, working men and grandmothers. I have been amazed to see the courage with which they take that walk into the unknown. All the men and women I have faced in that final moment convinced me that I have not prevented a single murder." Albert later told my dad that his one big regret was not being able to look Brady and Hindley in the eye, looking for some semblance of genuine remorse for the horrific murders they committed before he hooded them, slipped the rope around their necks and pulled the lever that sent them down to hell. A large sign above the bar read NO HANGING AROUND THE BAR, proof enough to me that Albert still retained a sense of humour as he looked back on his career, shaking my hand as we left the pub and leaving me thinking, now, is he left or right handed?

In Belfast during the summer of 1969, a series of violent, unprecedented, full scale riots broke out between Protestants and Catholics, the Orangemen purposely marching through Catholic dominated areas because they thought it was their God given right to march where they wanted, which agitated the Catholic population even more. As the riots intensified, the hopelessly undermanned Royal Ulster Constabulary was powerless to maintain any semblance of control, as three people were killed and scores more injured. In a passionate plea for help, the Irish Prime Minister telephoned the British Interior Minister James Callaghan for some urgent assistance, fearing a rising death toll was imminent. Callaghan met with Army generals, explaining the situation over in Belfast that was fast getting out of control, and the decision to send in the army was made. On the 14th of August 1969, under the codename Operation Banner, the first British troops arrived on the war torn streets of Belfast, and in sending them the generals in charge of assessing the worsening situation made a grave error. Instead of sending a run-of-the-mill regiment with no strong religious beliefs, they sent in the Scots Highlanders, who were staunch Protestants to a man, and who arrived in the ultra strong Nationalist Catholic stronghold of Andersons Town. Violence between the two sides quickly escalated. It has been said that a young Gerry Adams was watching everything through his bedroom window, deciding that what he was watching was not acceptable and that he was going to take up arms himself to fight for Ireland; and so the Troubles began.

A forty-year, bloody, violent episode in Irish history, leaving a litany of death and destruction, could so easily have been avoided if the generals had had some access to correct information and better planning. Official figures state that three thousand people were killed during the Troubles, fifty-two percent civilians, thirty-two percent military and sixteen percent paramilitaries. In response to the IRA, the Protestant loyalists created the Ulster Volunteer Force among other Protestant groups ready and willing to do battle with the IRA. A number of men within the UVF ranks rose to become the most terrifying, murdering, barbaric bunch of men ever to get involved with the Troubles. Two of the group's leaders, Lenny Murphy and Robert 'Basher' Bates, operated from the Mountjoy pub on the Shankhill Road, where they acquired the name of the Shankhill Butchers. Their hatred for Catholics was savage as they went about randomly kidnapping Catholics and taking them back to their base, which was the Lawnbrook Social Club, where the unfortunate victims were forcefully brought to be mercilessly tortured for days on end before they were killed. They were beaten half to death, throats slashed, teeth and fingernails wrenched from their body, and tortured with electric shocks before being chopped up with butcher's knives and hatchets. They killed twenty-three innocent people in the time they were active, with Lenny Murphy eventually killed by the IRA for his atrocious crimes.

TWO

Compared to the hedonism of the 1960s, the 70s were nothing short of a disaster, and they began with one of the worst incidents in the history of the Troubles. Utrinque Paratus - Ready For Anything - has been the regimental motto of the Parachute Regiment stretching back to the Second World War. Small wonder they regard themselves as the British Army's elite soldiers, next in line to the SAS, boasting a tough reputation for going in hard and asking questions later - and they certainly lived up to their reputation the day they were sent into Londonderry, on the 30th January 1972, with the aim of maintaining law and order amidst strong rumours that a large planned peace march would ignite into violence between Catholics and Protestants.

As tensions heightened between the protestors and the Paras, a number of hostile shots were reported to have been fired from one of the tower blocks. The Paras acted fast to get a grip on a worsening situation, opening fire in the direction where the alleged shots came from. In the terrible aftermath, the Paras shot twenty-six unarmed people, killing thirteen of them outright, with many suffering gunshot wounds to their backs while trying to run to safety. After searching the tower block where the supposed bullets were fired from, there was no trace of any spent cartridges. The Saville Report into the incident raised crucial damming evidence against the Paras, stating that the killings were unjustified and that the soldiers involved knowingly put forward false accounts of the day. Colonel Derek Wilford, the Commanding Officer of 1 Para on the day, was found to be partially responsible for the violence, telling his men not to stand cowering behind shelters like Aunt Sallies but to get out there like soldiers and get the rioters involved. He was later awarded the Order Of The British Empire and retired to rural France.

The massacre in the Bogside acted as a massive recruiting drive for the IRA as hundreds of young, fiercely patriotic Irish lads joined the cause. With General Gaddafi supplying them with unlimited arms and bomb making equipment, the IRA had gone from being a cottage industry to what many claimed back in the day was the most efficient terrorist organisation of the time, ready to wage all-out war on the Brits. As the campaign gathered momentum, bombs were going off all over Belfast city, killing many innocent people who had no part whatsoever in the bloodshed. It is incredible to discover that the Hotel Europa, the most famous hotel in Belfast and the favourite haunt of journalists and photographers covering the Troubles, was blown up and rebuilt and bombed again over thirty times.

With their unusual camouflaged Dennison Smocks and maroon berets, the Paras stood out on the streets of Belfast like a sore thumb, making them potential prime targets for any IRA gunman wanting to take revenge for the Bogside massacres. That meticulously planned revenge occurred on the 27th August 1979 at a place called Warrenpoint, where a number of heavily concealed IRA men from the South Armagh Brigade were ready and waiting to wreak total destruction on an unsuspecting convoy of Paras via two massive bombs. One six hundred pound bomb was hidden on a flatbed trailer and a second, weighing eight hundred pounds, was hidden in milk pails. As the soldiers drove past, the IRA blew up the bombs, instantly killing eighteen Paras and seriously wounding an additional twenty-three.

Official reports at the time described the the incident as sheer carnage, with many badly mutilated bodies strewn across the road and others hanging from trees. Lieutenant Colonel Corden Lloyd of the Royal Greenjackets was vaporised in the massive blast, and the only item that remained to help identify him was one of his tattered epaulettes. Mike Jackson, a Para officer, was called upon to help recognise his friend by what remained of his face, torn from his head by the intensity of the blast. As for the IRA men responsible for the bombing, they quietly slipped away, having more than avenged the deaths of those people killed in the Bogside. All told, thirty soldiers were killed, and the driver of one of the trucks, nineteen-year-old Anthony Wood, was found with his pelvis welded to the seat he was sitting on; but for the IRA men, the day wasn't over. Lord Louis Mountbatten, who lived in a castle, was out on his boat with two friends when the IRA blew it up with a large bomb stuck on the bottom of the hull. Mountbatten loved the Irish people and their country and to kill an old man like that just because he was connected to the hated British Royal Family was in my opinion totally unjustified, but as the old saying goes, all's fair in love and war.

Meanwhile, back on the beleaguered mainland, the situation in the country was rapidly deteriorating from bad to worse with a whole mountain of major problems to sort out that made us feel the country was falling apart. Oil prices went sky high thanks to the Arab Jewish Yom Kippur war and there was rising mass unemployment, abnormally high inflation, trade unions battling with the police under the strong leadership of Hugh Scanlon and Arthur Scargill, nationwide power cuts affecting all walks of life, increasing strikes by people who never usually resorted to striking to get their voices heard - nurses, grave diggers, garbage collectors and firemen leaving their job to the Army and their hopelessly antiquated Green Goddess fire engines to tackle any fires that might occur - the introduction of the three day working week, rising ethnic tensions between the allegedly racist police and civilians, increased IRA activity, including planting bombs in Britain - I mean, how much more could we as a nation take before the eventual slide into anarchy and despair? Faced with his country crumbling all around him, no wonder the Prime Minister Ted Heath took to sailing his boat to enjoy some precious time alone to give him space to come up with a remedy for the alarming decline across the country which he and his Conservative government appeared not to have a clue as to how they were going to sort the mess out.

Despite the daily doom and gloom we were all feeling, my parents and I managed to share some real tender moments, the likes of which we hadn't had for ages. The kitchen lit by several candles dotted around the room, their flickering choreography created a nice chilled-out mood as the three of us just sat there talking, laughing and listening to Ennio Morreconi Spaghetti Western themes, Mum cooking up Steak Canadians in barm cakes smothered in fried onions and mustard with some chips. After we finished the food we broke out the games for a couple of hours: Ludo, Cluedo, Snakes and Ladders, Monopoly and Snap and some game with a green plastic robot figure I forget the name of. Simple, enjoyable pleasures; Mum and Dad told me it felt like being back in the war as we had a good laugh, drinking a couple of glasses of Stones Ginger Wine before I hit the sack. Nights were spent under the blanket with a torch reading Paul Allen's Skinhead books and Sven Hassel's brilliant war time stories about fighting for the Germans on the Russian Front. Those early seventies proved to be extremely tough times for a lot of my mates who had been laid off with only the dole money to live on. Looking back, I was fortunate as my job being an apprentice was protected, meaning I got paid for the two days off work each week. Result!

The National Front was on the march in cities and towns across the country, with the outspoken party leader John Tyndall surrounded by a bodyguard of skinheads. Their strong presence gave real, genuine, non-racist skinheads a bad name - they wanted no part in politics, their only crime being that they liked drinking, a bit of speed, keeping their Doc Martens highly polished and dancing to West Indian ska music. Tyndall's right wing fascist speeches hit the mark with many disgruntled people who were deeply dismayed as to how the country seemed to be falling apart, not to mention the arrival of more and more coloured people. There was a large NF gathering taking place in Southall town hall on the 24th April 1979 which was causing great concern and anxiety for the locals, who feared that violence would break out.

As fully expected, loads of members of the Anti Nazi League turned up and a riot soon followed as the outnumbered police battled with the crowd. At some point in the day, a New Zealand teacher and activist called Blair Peach was killed, allegedly by a member of the Special Patrol Group, a special unit of bully boys Margaret Thatcher had created. Nobody was brought to justice for the murder because no evidence came forth. The SPG men looked identical in their riot gear, so nobody was charged, but one eye witness stated that "I saw policemen hitting people. People started to run away as the police tried to disperse them. I saw Peach and then I saw the policeman with the shield attack Peach." When a number of SPG men had their lockers searched, police found various offensive weapons, coshes, knives, hammers, and, in one locker, Nazi memorabilia, the owner of which claimed he was merely a militaria collector. Shortly after all the fuss had died down, the Special Patrol Group was disbanded.

The 1970s were dubbed the Golden Era of Football Hooliganism but for the life of me I never quite understood what was golden about getting your head kicked in at a football match. By far the worst group of supporters were the infamous Manchester United Red Army, of which I was a member for a time. Because of their sheer numbers, everywhere they went coppers and people braced themselves for the invasion. Thousands of teenagers in jeans and Doc Martens, scarves tied to their wrists, fighting with rival mobs. They came to Blackpool for a weekend to watch United away and held the town to ransom like they were above the law as they went on stealing sprees, getting drunk before returning home, leaving the town breathing one massive sigh of relief. I was on the Scoreboard End in Old Trafford in the early to mid 1970s when things suddenly got too nasty. One United fan threw a dart at the Leicester City goalkeeper that stuck in his neck, and that was enough for the government to take action. They ordered the Man United bosses to erect a steel safety fence around the ground. They were the first team in the football league to have this done. 'Caged Animals', the newspaper headlines read, but other grounds soon followed suit until people going to football learned to behave themselves in a civilised manner.

I can't recall exactly how long the power cuts lasted but I have a vague idea that the lights went out around eight o'clock in the evening, forcing me to come up with a cunning plan to beat the power cuts. I stocked up on batteries, spending hours taping my favourite music on my trusty portable Sanyo cassette recorder. I made sure my Tilly storm lamp was topped up with methylated spirits, with a few candles to give the room a bit of a nice moody atmosphere. I prepared a tray with a kettle, a jug of water, mug and spoon, some sugar and milk, a quarter bottles of Bells whisky for a nightcap and for the munchies a packet of Scotch shortbread, a couple of packets of salt and vinegar crisps and a couple of mint Aeros. I've always been into music as far back as I can remember. One particular Christmas, Dad, having arrived back from his travels in South Africa, gave me a fabulous present. It appeared to be a shiny black and chrome attaché case - they were very popular at the time - but this one was different. It opened up into a portable music centre comprising a record deck, amplifier and radio, with the lid opening out to a pair of speakers courtesy of Crown Electronics, making me feel like I was James Bond every time I opened it up to spin a few sounds. The other present he gave me that day was an EP containing my four favourite television theme tunes, *Captain Scarlet*, *Stingray*, *Thunderbirds* and *Fireball XL5*.

My first big musical influence came from the Spencer Davis Group, from Birmingham, boasting a four man line up of Spencer Davis on guitar, Pete York, and two brothers, Steve and Muff Winwood, on keyboards, guitar and bass respectively. They had a driving, energetic sound that I later equated to being similar to northern soul, producing classics like 'Somebody Help Me', 'I'm A Man', 'Keep On Runnin' and 'Gimme Some Lovin' - a really powerful British band, steeped in the kind of American rhythm and blues I later lived and breathed. Apart from the album *Let It Be*, I was never into The Beatles, The Stones or The Who, but I did like The Byrds, a lot of early Rod Stewart and the Small Faces, the darlings of the swinging 60s London scene featuring Steve Marriott, Ronnie Lane, Kenny Jones, and Jimmy Wilson, who was later replaced by Ian McLagan, writing catchy songs like 'Watcha Gonna Do About It', 'All Or Nothing', 'Sha La La La La', 'Itchycoo Park' and 'Lazy Sunday Afternoon', all brilliant 60s classics I still play today when the mood grabs me.

I loved The Kinks as well, mainly due to the fact that they had their own recognisable sound and their songs were quintessentially English, reflecting down-to-earth life so well. 'Autumn Almanac', 'Sunny Afternoon', 'Dedicated Follower of Fashion', 'Waterloo Sunset', 'Death Of A Clown', 'You Really Got Me', 'Till The End Of The Day' and 'Lola' describing a mixed up, muddled, shook up world, and who would argue with that when the binary non-binary crowd are doing their best to convince little boys to be girls and vice versa. Other music I was well into included Bowie, Roxy, Leonard Cohen, Cat Stevens, Slade, Thin Lizzy, Rory Gallagher, Dusty Springfield, Ronnie Scott, Tubby Hayes, Stan Getz, Dexter Gordon, Lester Young, Chet Baker and Miles Davis. Of course all that changed the morning I walked into Woolworths department store and heard this fabulous storming soul record blasting out from the speakers. The counter assistant told me that it was called '25 Miles' by a Motown artist called Edwin Starr and that was that for me. My record collection came under two different categories: Pre Tamla and Post Tamla. I soon started getting a decent collection of singles together from Motown, Stax and Atlantic artists. Also I had a few of the brilliant Tamla Motown LPs *Motown Chartbusters* featuring a cool selection of artists which represented really good value for money, considering that many of the artists were already established names.

Those of us who were on the northern soul scene back then were young and ambitious, and the impossible was anything but. We could never have known that the scene would become Britain's oldest surviving largely underground music scene, which owes its amazing longevity to a fanatical bunch of deejays and record collectors who used to make regular trips to all parts of America sifting through warehouses, record shops and second-hand shops. They went anywhere and everywhere searching for original rhythm and blues singles, the rarer the better, to bring back to Britain, where they unleashed all their latest finds on the unsuspecting northern soul faithful.

Records that cost a few shillings in the States back then would eventually sell for hundreds and often thousands of pounds as the years slipped by and these records became that much harder to find. One record in particular became the ultimate 'souly grail' for all serious vinyl junkies to own. Back in the 1960s, Berry Gordy, who was the founder of Tamla Motown, gave an obscure sound engineer called Frank Wilson his shot at fame and fortune, writing and producing just one single, called 'Do I Love You Indeed I Do'. As the story goes, three hundred copies of the single were pressed, out of which only three are reputed to exist, making the single the rarest, most valuable northern soul single in the world. So much so that a couple of years ago, a wealthy young entrepreneur and soul music fan from the Midlands shelled out a cool one hundred and twenty-five thousand - some say one hundred and fifty thousand - pounds for the privilege of owning a record that turned out to become an iconic moment in soul music history.

Staying much closer to home, walk into most bars and clubs across Britain and the chances are you will find a soul night, but back in the 1970s it was a much more elusive beast to find. You had to know where you were you looking, a few words in the right ear, a knock on the right door, seconds after which a slot would slide back as a pair of discerning eyes decided if you were cool enough to enter the nocturnal underworld, where you were greeted by strange, unfamiliar faces that eventually became loyal, lifelong friends, sharing a passion for the music and the scene that came with a warning: one bite and you were hooked for life, with no known antidote. Surrounded by a sheer wall of constant hopelessness and uncertainty, my friends and I threw ourselves headlong into the northern soul nights taking place in Blackpool and Wigan Casino every weekend. The club quickly became our temporary home from home where we all left our troubles and strife outside, leaving us to share a few precious hours in the company of similar minded people who felt more like family than friends. Wigan Casino gave us the chance to block out the reality of our lives, at least until eight o'clock the following morning when the final record played out. Shaking hands, hugging and kissing with firm promises to see you all next Saturday for sure for more of the same, we said our goodbyes and headed home to face another miserable week. We had a popular saying within the ranks of the northern soul scene that is as relevant today as it was to all of us back then, consisting of three simple words: Keep The Faith, because many times during our lives, facing the good with the bad when it looks like we have no way out, faith is the only remaining meaningful thing we all have left to pull us through.

My accidental introduction to the northern soul scene occurred in Blackpool in the spring of 1974. Although the 70s were grim, me and my mates still enjoyed ourselves come the weekend. I mean, we were living in Blackpool after all, so what was there not to enjoy? I was at my adolescent peak with a wardrobe full of all the tastiest mod related clobber: Ben Sherman and Brutus shirts, Fred Perry tops, Wrangler and Levi jeans, Slazenger jumpers, Sta Prest chinos, a sheepskin, two Harringtons, a Crombie style overcoat and a smart black Baranthea blazer with footwear courtesy of Doc Marten, Loakes brogues and loafers and Clarks suede desert boots with a couple of suits I got made up at Jacksons The Tailor, a nationwide chain of clothing manufacturers similar to Burtons and John Colliers. Not half as expensive as proper tailor-made suits but still quality clothing for an affordable price.

Getting a suit made up at Jacksons was quite a civilised, friendly experience, with the staff going all out to make the customers feel that little bit special. First you were measured up before sitting down to choose what cloth you wanted, from sober, subtle colours to eccentric checks and loud pinstripes, from a large bible-sized book of material offcuts. Jackets single or double breasted, four or six buttons, patch or flap pockets, with or without a rear vent and possibly a waistcoat, trousers tapered or loose fitting with or without turn ups, button or zip flies and waist adjusters as well as sewn creases or pleats. After all that you'd pay a small deposit in return for a weekly paying-in book, five pounds a month more or less, and that was that. A month or so later you'd receive confirmation that your suit was in the shop waiting for you to pick it up; a final try on to make sure everything fitted in all the right places, which for me it did every time, then race back home after some fish, chips and peas with a few cans of Strongbow and I'd be in the bath soaking away the crap of another building site week before slipping on my latest suit of armour, shaving, a splash of Brut 33 and hair slicked back courtesy of some Vaseline hair tonic and I'd be off for the night feeling like Steve McQueen in *The Thomas Crown Affair*, dying to show off my new suit to my mates before another mental night on the seaside merry-go-round.

My weekend staple diet of football, pubs and clubs was wearing thin with me. I needed to find a new scene, which was about the time I kept seeing this bunch of cool lads on scooters buzzing about here and there, who I found out called themselves the Okeh Crew, so named after the highly respected northern soul record label of the same name. A mate of mine had already joined them and was having a great time so I needed no more convincing. A week or so later I was down at John Halls, the local bike and scooter dealer, where I purchased a brand new Lambretta GP 150 in white with black stripes plus an assortment of bolt-on accessories, front and back crash bars, front bumper, spare wheel carrier, a folding Bermuda backrest and perspex bubble flyscreen that came to around two hundred quid if memory serves me correctly.

They were a great bunch of lads, who owned some fantastic individual style scooters, each with their wooden heraldic shield fixed to the back of their scooters, or chairs as we called them. Having your own shield meant that you were now a fully fledged member of the Okeh Scooter Crew, of which I was an extremely proud member the day I was presented with my shiny purple and white shield with my name on, fixed to the back of my Lammy. Even now, more than fifty years since the Okeh Crew were operating, my total undying respect goes out to two of the founding members of the original crew, Paul Livesey and his trusted wingman Kev McKay, both still as passionate about scooters as they've ever been, completing what must have been a long, tiring journey to Italy and back as well as finding the time to run the Blackpool Soul Club, both of them fully determined to keep the faith burning bright and strong forever.

It was the Okeh Scooter Crew that was responsible for my chance introduction to the strange nocturnal world of northern soul. A different nightclub, a different deejay playing different music and my life would have been a whole lot more happy, fulfilled and worthwhile than it is today, but what is life if not predictable? You pay your money and you take your choice, with no going back. One Saturday night early in 1974 we went up to a club called Gallopers, a few miles from Blackpool, where a well-respected deejay called Pete Haigh was the man behind the decks. He's still spinning the sounds today, doing what he does best. The club was the kind of commercial place where hippies, skinheads, mods, glam rockers, heavy rockers, Bowie and Roxy freaks all had their fifteen minutes of dancefloor fun.

After things had quietened down somewhat, Pete played this one particular track of music that literally blew me away as well as providing me with my first real introduction to the magical world of northern soul. It was a song by an artist called Jerry Williams, singing a powerful love song called 'If You Ask Me' that I soon had in my rapidly expanding collection of northern soul singles. A really beautiful love story of one man singing his heart out to the woman he adores like no other, telling her that if she asks him, then he will do anything to please her. Pete was good enough to have a chat with me after the last record, telling me all about this wonderful music that started out as rhythm and blues before being renamed northern soul. He put me right after I asked him where I could get my hands on some northern soul singles: a shop called Melody House in Bond Street, Blackpool, and an even better shop called Synfonia Records on Cookson Street in the town centre, the place I ended up spending countless hours in listening to the owner, Sandie Mountain, educating me on this fabulous new music I'd discovered in the confines of his well-stocked back room.

Going to Sandie's shop was an experience never forgotten. Saturday morning up early, jump in the bath before getting dressed and shooting off into town to meet my mates for a full English fry-up, then heading up to Sandie's with my list of titles I wanted to buy. Sandie was a gentle, softly spoken, unassuming spirit with a knowledge of northern soul/rhythm and blues music second to none. Scooters parked up outside with military precision, the inside of the shop packed with older lads, Ben Shermans, sheepskins, Levis, Doc Martens, loafers and brogues with me the young soul apprentice wedged somewhere between them. The interior of the shop was nothing less than totally chaotic. Singles and LPs all over the floor or stacked in precarious tower blocks on the counter and yet through all the endless confusion, Sandie could put his hand on any single ordered by a customer in seconds, like he had some weird sixth sense. If I didn't know the title of a record I'd heard at Wigan, all I would have to do was hum the chorus and he'd disappear briefly into the back room, appearing seconds later with the single.

The other guy who boasted a reputation of being the country's first ever record dealer was called Garry Wilde. He owned a tobacconist kiosk in Victoria Street in the town centre; hardly the place you would imagine buying rare soul records from, but Garry had a special shelf in his kiosk for just such an occasion and often you'd see clusters of mods checking out the latest soul sounds like some weird East meets West *Funeral In Berlin* scenario. He often charged a fiver a single for some of the rarer records he was selling. There were three great venues in Blackpool responsible for playing some class northern soul sounds. We had the Highland Room, a club needing no introduction, being one of the most respected clubs on the scene. Then there was the

Peacock Room in the Cherry Tree pub, where a lot of the scooter lads used to congregate, and then my favourite venue, the large room inside the Blackpool Casino, a wonderful white curved Art Deco extravaganza built in front of the Pleasure Beach that is still there today, thank God. The music played in there was second to none, thanks to the deejays, Garry Wilde and the inimitable, super friendly Mister Baz Stanton RIP, who instinctively knew what records to play in order to keep the dancefloor full. Later on, when I was going to Wigan, the Casino would be the meeting place where we sorted out all the nitty gritty business before shooting off to Wigan: who was going, did they have a car, who needed a lift and was there any gear - amphetamine - knocking about, and if so, how much.

Around early 1973, a well known, respectable local entrepreneur club owner called Pete Schofield opened up what he called Scoeys, which at the time was well different to anything else in town. Three floors, if I remember right, furnished with sofas and armchairs, catering for different music lovers. They had a Bowie Roxy room, a room for rock freaks and the top room for northern soulies. Sunday mornings, relaxing, coming down from the previous night's speed, we were spaced out on sofas and chairs like in a living room. Scoeys was only a short lived venture but it was a cool place to spend some time in with good mates. It was the place where I first heard mention of the Wigan Casino, some old ballroom in Wigan that was putting on some brilliant all-nighters, so people who were regulars told us; they said we should check it out for ourselves. I thought nothing of it and the reality of spending a whole night in a run down ballroom held no appeal; but funny how things can change when you least expect them to. One time in Scoeys I saw a notice: 'Coach leaving for Wigan Casino two weeks' time. Spaces left and a membership card a must.' Just a simple, unobtrusive note that had an air of mystery to it, which changed my life forever; and once again the rest is history.

THREE

In the late eighteen hundreds and early nineteen hundreds in America, an unexpected economic disaster occurred, rapidly becoming so widespread that it was solely responsible for destroying the Southern States' entire crop of cotton, costing millions of dollars as well as causing long term high unemployment. The cause of this almost biblical plague was an airborne beetle called the boll weevil. Each spring they attacked the cotton plants by injecting their eggs into the plant, after which it would be destroyed. They were voracious eaters and soon the economy of the South plummeted into a steep decline, almost to the point of bankruptcy, forcing farmers to turn to the new peanut crop, which was impervious to the beetle.

What has the boll weevil plague got to do with a book on soul music? Well, might I dare suggest that if it wasn't for the boll weevil epidemic, then we might not have rhythm and blues music. Because of the high unemployment and there being no cotton to pick, vast numbers of black Americans packed up their belongings and headed for the industrial centres of Chicago, Detroit, Kansas, Los Angeles, New York and Memphis in search of regular work. This massive movement of people was called the Great Migration and occurred between 1916 and 1936, followed by a second Great Migration from 1941 through to 1950, when the demand for labour went through the roof as a result of the Second World War, at about the time when the new rhythm and blues music began to get popular. The huge black American musical influence not only helped to establish the music but was also a contributing factor in breaking down the centuries-old, bitter racial differences as white youths flocked to the clubs to listen to the new sounds and dance the night away. In Los Angeles alone a large, vibrant entertainment scene grew, with the city boasting eight new record labels specialising in the all-new rhythm and blues music.

In 1916 the Smithsonian Institute published a paper describing rhythm and blues music as follows - "A distinctly African American music drawing from the deep south tributaries of African American expressive culture. It is an infectious amalgam of of jump blues, swing, gospel, blues and boogie woogie that initially developed over three decades that bridged an era of legally sanctioned racial segregation, international conflicts and the struggle for civil rights." Powerful, evocative words echoing centuries of pain and suffering of the African people. Dragged from their loved ones, stripped, chained up and packed like sardines into the hulls of notorious slave ships like the *Amistad*, facing a life of unimaginable cruelty and servitude at the hands of their wealthy masters and mistresses. Their only relief from the constant pain and misery was playing crude home made instruments on the porches of their ramshackle cabins, watching the sun going down and hoping and praying for a better day. That day finally came when the North beat the South in a bloody civil war, costing the lives of over one million five hundred thousand men dying for what they believed in; and so began a rich, constantly changing tapestry of black American music that has developed into a multi billion dollar music genre in its own right.

A typical band set up would comprise one piano, one or two guitars, a bass, a saxophone and drums, often featuring backing singers to spread the icing on a very sweet cake indeed. To mark out their new territory, the band members would often appear wearing smart suits, while others took things one step further by wearing uniforms. During the twenties and thirties, new black American stars were born, with guys like Cab Calloway, Louis Jordan, Lonnie Johnson, T Bone Walker and Count Basie. Louis

Jordan soon established himself as one of the main artists on the rhythm and blues scene, playing with a band called The Tympany Five, featuring himself on saxophone backed up by a second horn, a trumpet, a bass and piano and drums. In 1948 Louis Jordan's music claimed the top five places on the rhythm and blues chart but other stars were also emerging like Big Joe Turner, Roy Brown, and Wynonie Harris making names for themselves.

In 1949 'The Hucklebuck' topped the charts for almost one year with a band fronted by saxophonist Paul Williams and a song that many people described as downright risqué and dirty, causing audiences to explode into a frenzy of rioting in a number of venues across America that were eventually closed down. The same year saw Jimmy Witherspoon take the number one spot with his single 'Ain't Nobody's Business' alongside Louis Jordan's hit 'Saturday Night Fish Fry'. The demand for these records was massive, so much so that new rhythm and blues recording labels were being set up to cope with the demand like Savoy, King, Chess, Imperial and Atlantic.

Despite its growing popularity, initial sales of these records were largely confined to black audiences, with barely any white sales or access to radio shows. This suddenly changed in the nineteen fifties as more and more white teenagers started to get into rhythm and blues music. In a clear indication of just how popular the new music was becoming, Dolphins record store in Hollywood reported that over forty percent of all record sales went to white kids. In 1951, Johnny Otis was enjoying a lot of success with three of his hit singles, 'Cupid's Boogie', 'Double Crossing Blues' and 'Mistrustin' Blues', each single claiming the number one spot.

Also the same year saw the arrival of the one and only Little Richard, who was signed to RCA records, playing the forties rhythm and blues. Three years later he was asked to do a demo that shot him to fame and fortune almost overnight. The record was called 'Tutti Frutti', a record attracting big interest from Speciality Records that redefined the sound of rock and roll. This was quickly followed by 'Long Tall Sally' and the rest, as we all know, is musical history.

Soul singer Ruth Brown, who was often described as the queen of rhythm and blues, was signed to Atlantic records and between 1951 and 1954 managed to have several hits in the top five charts every year. Fats Domino was also in the charts, along with Ray Charles with 'I Got A Woman', with his unique blend of spiritual and blues music. Bo Diddley recorded 'Maybelline' for Chess records, going on to claim the number three spot on the rhythm and blues chart as well as an incredible entry into the top thirty pop charts. Such was the powerful influence of rhythm and blues music that *Rolling Stone* magazine once stated that "all people black and white were mentally influenced by rhythm and blues music." A selection of RnB artists, including Chuck Berry, Al Hibbler, Cathy Carr and the delectable Della Reese, undertook a tour of America visiting Columbia, South Carolina, Annapolis, Pennsylvania, Rochester, Pittsburgh, Syracuse and New York. In Annapolis alone, such was the frenzy to see the shows that police reported traffic jams as well as between fifty and sixty thousand people trying desperately to squeeze into an eight thousand seat cinema, resulting in many kids getting badly injured.

1959 marked the arrival of two black owned record labels, Sam Cooke's Sar label and Berry Gordy's mighty Tamla Motown, which became the biggest successful record label going. Bill Black, Elvis Presley's former bass player and the frontman to Bill Black's Combo, which scored a massive hit on the northern soul scene with the storming instrumental 'Little Queenie', was starting to attract large black audiences. This was backed up by the fact that some ninety percent of all his record sales were being bought by black people. His incredible success occurred because people thought that he was actually a black artist because his sound was so funky and black influenced.

By the early nineteen sixties, rhythm and blues music had taken America by storm and was renamed soul music, with the name 'blue eyed soul' applying to whites who preferred playing soul music. Motown enjoyed its first ever million-selling single in 1960 with 'Shop Around' by the Miracles. A year later and it was the mighty Stax label that scored its first major hit thanks to Carla Thomas and the single 'Gee Whizz Look At His Eyes', followed by a second hit courtesy of the Mar Keys instrumental 'Last Night'. Little Richard, Jerry Butler, Chuck Jackson, Little Milton, Johnny Guitar Watson, Aretha Franklin, Sam Cooke, Ruth Brown, Fats Domino, The Drifters, Ray Charles, Big Joe Turner, Etta James, Jackie Wilson, Isley Brothers, Ben E King, Johnny Otis, The Clovers, Little Anthony and the Imperials, Bo Diddley, Brook Benton, Jimmy Witherspoon, Lee Dorsey, Lavern Baker - these are just a selection of the wonderful, visionary artists who contributed so much to help establish rhythm and blues music become established back in the early days. With the population of America firmly under control of rhythm and blues' driving beats and passionate vocals, it was time to turn its attention to the British market, hoping to create the same kind of success it was enjoying across America but also fully aware that the British market might prove to be a tougher one to break into. Time would tell.

It was the hugely respected former music journalist and legendary music producer Jerry Wexler who first coined the phrase 'Rhythm and Blues' and so it is only right and fitting that this story features the guy whose contribution to American music was immeasurable. Jerry was born on January 10th 1917 in the Bronx to a German Jewish father and Polish Jewish mother. He served in the army, after which he graduated from the University of Kansas with a degree in journalism. Jerry's early career began with him working for the prestigious music magazine *Billboard* as a writer, editor and reporter. Up until 1949, all African American music was labelled under the name 'race music', a title that didn't fit well with Jerry's feelings at the time. "Race was a common term then. A self referral used by blacks. Race records didn't sit well with me. I came up with a handle I thought that suited the music well. Rhythm and Blues. It was a label more appropriate to more enlightened times."

In 1953, Jerry changed direction when he went to work for Atlantic Records and singlehandedly transformed the label into the success it is today. He worked with many artists including Wilson Pickett, Aretha Franklin and our very own queen of soul, the one the only Dusty Springfield, producing her acclaimed album *Live in Memphis*. 1979 saw Jerry switching his allegiance from Atlantic to Warner Records with an early success by producing Bob Dylan's first album, *Slow Train Coming*. Of all the artists he worked with, for me personally, Jerry's greatest contribution to the music industry and soul fans across the world was him saving the career of Aretha Franklin. Before meeting Jerry, Aretha was signed to Columbia Records and her career seemed to all intents and purposes to be heading in the right direction with several hit singles including 'One Step Ahead', 'Cry Like A Baby' and 'You Made Me Love You'. These were backed up by numerous live shows and television appearances. However, failing record sales and the fact that she owed Columbia Records a lot of money caused a slump in her career. At the crucial moment, when all seemed to be lost, Jerry Wexler stepped in, managing to convince Aretha to ditch Columbia and sign for Atlantic. She did; and the rest is history. Somehow, in the relationship shared with Aretha, Columbia Records failed to recognise her strong gospel music background, which she had been singing since she was a young girl. Jerry saw this as a vital ingredient to any future success she hoped to achieve. Under

Jerry's guidance a new Aretha Franklin rose from the ashes, a talented pianist in her own right who combined elements of gospel, blues and jazz in her music to create a new, instantly recognisable soul sound she claimed as her own. Hit after hit followed for Aretha as she consolidated her claim to being the queen of soul. The single 'I Never Loved A Man The Way I Love You' stormed to number one on the RnB chart and number nine on the *Billboard* Hot 100. Shortly after this, Aretha sang an Otis Redding song that she made her own, which became not only a Civil Rights anthem but a prayer for feminists across the world, as Otis commented later:" That little girl done took my song away from me." That song was 'Respect', and two more singles followed in its wake, 'Baby I Love You' and 'You Make Me Feel Like A Natural Woman'.

More success followed, with the release of three new albums, *I Never Loved A Man The Way I Love you*, *Lady Soul* and *Aretha*, which spawned the hit singles 'Chain Of Fools', 'Ain't No Way' and her all time classic 'Say A Little Prayer For Me'. These singles earned her two Grammys and a Best Female RnB Vocal Performance in 1968. Sadly, the undisputed queen of soul left us for that great recording studio in the sky when she passed away in 2013 from a malignant pancreatic cancer at the age of seventy-six. For her lifetime contribution to both the music industry and the Civil Rights movement, Aretha Franklin was recognised with numerous awards. She was first on the *Rolling Stone* magazine list of the one hundred greatest singers of all time and ninth on their one hundred greatest artists of all time. 2012 saw her inducted into the Gospel Music Hall of Fame. Further acclaim came from *Rolling Stone* both in 2002 and 2012 with her album *I Never Loved A Man The Way I Love You* voted number one two times. In 2015 *Billboard* voted her the greatest female RnB artist of all time and in 2018 she was inducted into the Memphis Music Hall of Fame.

In 2015, Barack Obama paid tribute to her with the following words:" Nobody embodies more fully the connection between the African American spiritual, the blues, RnB and rock 'n' roll the way that hardship and sorrow were transformed into something full of beauty and vitality and hope. American history wells up when Aretha sings. That's why when she sits down at a piano and sings 'A Natural Woman', she can move me to tears the same way the Ray Charles version of 'America The Beautiful' will always be in my view the most patriotic piece of music ever performed because it captures the fullness of the American experience. The view from the bottom as well as the top, the good and the bad and the possibility of synthesis, reconciliation and transcendence."

Jerry Wexler's lifelong contribution to the music industry was justly recognised when he was inducted into the Hall of Fame in 1987. He remained in his beloved New York for most of his life, his latter years sharing a home with a Chinese family up until he died in 2008 from heart failure at the age of ninety-one. I really liked his sarcastic reply to a question a film maker once asked him:" Hey Jerry, what words are you going to have on your tombstone?" Jerry simply replied with "Two words: more bass." Thank you so much Mister Jerry Wexler on behalf of all true soul fans around the world, who owe it to you for saving Aretha Franklin at a troubled time in her career when she could so easily have faded into obscurity eternal.

FOUR

Thankfully it isn't just in times of war that the United Kingdom and America have remained staunch allies. Since the 1960s, they have shared a deep mutual appreciation of music. Promoters on both sides of the pond quickly caught on to the idea of staging large outdoor music festivals featuring the very best bands and artists from both countries. From 1967 through to 1970 a string of massive music festivals that laid the foundations for things to come attracted thousands of fans to come and listen to what was on offer, as well as providing them with the chance to lose themselves for a few days in the whole 'turn on, tune in and drop out' sex, drugs and rock and roll philosophy as preached by Timothy Leary, who first announced his new world vision in 1967 when he appeared in front of thirty thousand tripped out hippies at the Human Be-In festival held in San Francisco's Golden Gate Park.

1967 saw the Monterey International Pop Festival, at which some fifty thousand people turned up to watch the Grateful Dead, Janis Joplin, Otis Redding, Jimi Hendrix, Jefferson Airplane, Buffalo Springfield, Canned Heat and the Mamas and the Papas.

1968 saw the Newport Pop Festival with some one hundred thousand people who'd come to watch The Byrds, Steppenwolf, Tiny Tim, The James Cotton Blues Band and Quicksilver Messenger Service.

Once again in 1968 saw the Miami Pop Festival pulling in ninety thousand people to watch Fleetwood Mac, Chuck Berry, Buffe Sainte Marie, Steppenwolf, Richie Havers, Marvin Gaye, Joni Mitchell, The McCoy's, Junior Walker and the All Stars, Joe Tex, the Grateful Dead, the Turtles, Sweetwater and Flat and Scruggs.

1969 saw the Newport Festival attract one hundred and fifty thousand people to watch Ike and Tina Turner, the Rascals, Johnny Winter, Jethro Tull, Eric Burden, The Byrds, Booker T and the MG's, Jimi Hendrix, Creedence Clearwater Revival, Spirit and Taj Mahal. Again in 1969 Newport hosted the Jazz Festival, attended by over seventy thousand people to watch Jeff Beck, Led Zeppelin, Ten Years After, Blood Sweat and Tears, Jethro Tull and James Brown.

1969 also saw the Atlantic Pop Festival attended by one hundred and ten thousand people, there to see Spirit, Chicago, Joe Cocker, the Staple Singers, Led Zeppelin, Canned Heat, Creedence Clearwater Revival, Johnny Winter and Ian and Sylvia, the Chamber Brothers, Arthur Brown, Janis Joplin, Doctor John, Three Dog Night, Little Richard, Procol Harum, BB King, Jefferson Airplane, Joni Mitchell and Iron Butterfly.

1969 also saw the Woodstock Festival attended by more than four hundred thousand people to watch The Who, Melanie, the Grateful Dead, Jimi Hendrix, Johnny Winter, Ten Years After, Joe Cocker, Joan Baez, Crosby Stills Nash and Young, Arlo Guthrie, Jefferson Airplane, Blood Sweat and Tears, The Incredible String Band, John Sebastian, Joe and the Fish, Sly and the Family Stone, The Band, Santana, Canned Heat, Sweetwater, Sha Na Na and Tim Hardin.

1969 also saw the Texas International Pop Festival attracting one hundred and twenty thousand people to watch Santana, Spirit, Tony Joe White, Sweetwater, Chicago, Janis Joplin, Johnny Winter, Nazz, Sam and Dave, Grand Funk Railroad, Led Zeppelin, The Incredible String Band, Delaney and Bonnie and Rotary Convention.

1969 also saw the Altamont Festival attracting some three hundred thousand people who'd come to watch the Rolling Stones, Jefferson Airplane, Santana, Crosby Stills Nash and Young, and the Flying Burrito Brothers. Tragically the Altamont Festival qualifies as the blackest day in American music festival history. For such a large event, the actual stage area was small, with barely enough room for the bands to perform on, as well as raising concerns that the people in front of the crowd could be in a dangerous position if a stage invasion occurred. The festival organisers needed a solution and fast. In view of this problem it's claimed by many that Mick Jagger hired members of the Oakland chapter of the notorious Hell's Angels motorcycle gang to police the event. They agreed, and their price for doing this was a mere five hundred dollars' worth of beer.

With the Angels protecting the stage area, violence broke out when some people tried to get on the stage. Women were seen to be thrown off the stage by their hair and one man, Meredith Hunter, was stabbed to death with a sharpened motorcycle spoke by Hell's Angel Alan Passaro. Three more people were killed in hit and run incidents and one person drowned in a nearby canal. Alan Passaro was arrested and charged with murder but later released when police studied a video of the incident clearly showing Meredith Hunter, who at the time was completely off his head on methamphetamine, pull out a gun, pointing it at Mick Jagger. Passaro reacted fast, jumping on Hunter to prevent him from killing Jagger.

Switching to the United Kingdom, 1970 was the year of the five day festival on the Isle of Wight attended by a staggering six hundred thousand people to watch Leonard Cohen, Joan Baez, Procol Harum, The Who, The Doors, Joni Mitchell, Jimi Hendrix, Supertramp, and Chicago. 1970 saw the first Glastonbury Festival, attended by only one thousand five hundred people, there to watch Roy Harper, T Rex, Ian Anderson, Steam Hammer, Wayne Fontana, Amazing Blondel, Stackridge and Keith Christmas. Glastonbury is now a globally established annual music event attracting thousands of festival goers. This year over two hundred thousand people attended the event. each paying £360 a ticket, making a grand total of £71 million. Not bad for a few days' work once a year.

1960s America wasn't just about acid, dope, free love and music. In my opinion what took place at the Altamont festival incident symbolised what was an extremely turbulent, violent time in American history. Despite thousands upon thousands of black Americans leaving the Southern States for good, equally so thousands of brothers and sisters both young and old had chosen to remain living in the Southern States for fear of change, despite having a terrible time of things, similar in so many ways to Adolf Hitler and the way he actively persecuted the Jews in 1930s Germany. Looking back now it's truly disgusting to read about how black people were treated, completely segregated from all normal walks of life during the 1950s and 1960s, forbidden to do things that white folks took for granted. Inter race marriages were banned. Bosses and businessmen kept white and black clientele apart, as was the case in restaurants that had separate bathroom facilities for blacks and whites. Buses and trains had separate seating while hospitals had separate entrances and treatment rooms. Dead blacks were banned from being buried next to a white grave and they were even banned from playing basketball. Theatres had separate places for black audiences and any white person found to be renting property to black people could be fined up to one hundred dollars and possibly jailed for up to sixty days; and so the restrictions continued.

It took the actions of one extremely courageous woman called Rosa Parks to stand up and say "I have had enough." Rosa lived in Montgomery, a place noted for its violence against black people, but regardless Rosa was determined to make her mark and make clear that she was just as equal a person as anybody else. Despite possible terrible repercussions she knew she'd face, Rosa adamantly refused to surrender her bus seat to a white person, causing her to be arrested and put on trial. Her bravery went on to inspire many blacks to join her, prompting increasing numbers daring to enter restaurants, bars and cinemas, sitting in seats usually reserved for the white folks.

The rapidly worsening situation was like a powder keg just waiting to explode, and explode it did in towns across the Southern States with large numbers of black people out for violence taking to the streets. They were hopelessly outnumbered and ill equipped to face the government's response, which was to send in the police, army and National Guard, who beat them mercilessly before turning on the powerful water cannons the black protestors were no match for, as we see in footage of them being swept off their feet down the roads by the powerful jets of water. It was around the time when a group calling themselves the Black Panthers were seen in public, prompting J Edgar Hoover, head of the FBI, to call them the greatest threat to America's national security.

With only some two thousand members, willing to die for the cause, they appointed themselves the armed wing of the growing peace movement whose leader and spokesman was Dr Martin Luther King, a baptist minister, activist and philosopher who called for strictly peaceful protests as opposed to taking up arms. The Panthers' leader was a powerful influential political activist called Malcolm X, leader of the Nation of Islam, who called on his members to take more militant action against the white racists. They wore military style uniforms, black berets, black leather jackets, black trousers and boots which gave them a striking appearance. In the 1968 Mexico Olympics, athletes Tommie Smith and John Carlos were on the podium to receive their gold and silver medals, after which they raised one arm each, wearing black leather gloves, their fists clenched in defiance as to the horrors of what was happening to black people in the deep South, a striking image that no doubt drove J Edgar Hoover to distraction.

Meanwhile the Peace Movement under the leadership of Dr King was growing at an alarming rate, with white people standing alongside blacks calling for an end to violence and segregation. In many States, the Ku Klux Klan attracted many new members, white redneck racist supremacists who passionately believed that they were the saviours of white America, gathering around their burning crosses dressed in their ridiculous white pointed hats and gowns. The Klan was founded in 1870 and represented in almost every Southern State. Its members were absolutely dedicated to the idea of total white supremacy. As the campaign for equal rights gathered momentum, the Klan responded by bombing a number of black schools and churches. In South Carolina, a well known Klan stronghold, it was reported that around five hundred masked men attacked a prison and lynched eight black inmates.

Judged by many as a lunatic fringe group, the Klan were in fact a highly secretive, well organised group with some powerful members and access to firearms come the day when they went to war for white America. During this worrying time they took it upon themselves to go out hunting for black people and those caught were subject to torture and beating before being lynched and their bodies set on fire. A powerful emotional poem that symbolised the terrible treatment black people suffered at the time was 'Strange Fruit', written by Jewish composer Abel Meeropol and sung by Billie Holliday.

In 1963 the Peace Movement was at its most powerful and to show the government just how powerful the movement had become, a quarter of a million people, blacks and whites together, marched to Washington, where they heard Dr King give his incredibly moving "I have a dream" speech to the assembled masses. It was one of the greatest speeches ever performed. After a long hard fight against all odds, the Peace Movement made history. In 1964 the Civil Rights Act was passed, followed by the Voting Rights Act in 1965 and three years later the Fair Housing Act. In the same year Martin Luther King, John F Kennedy and Malcolm X were assassinated by persons unknown, unless you just happened to be the FBI chief J Edgar Hoover, who knew a lot more about the killings than was ever proved.

Given all that tumultuous struggle for equal rights for all Americans, it certainly wasn't the ideal time for a young black guy starting out with a dream of owning America's biggest recording company, but through everything Berry Gordy somehow managed to find a bridge over troubled waters, prompting him to move his family to Detroit. It was a city he always had a deep affinity for, naming his record label after it - Motown - Motor City - Tamla Motown - and once again history was made. With only a mere eight hundred dollars to his name, Berry bought a detached building on 2468 West Boulevard. He converted the upstairs into an apartment to house his family while downstairs served as a makeshift recording studio in the building that the world would eventually come to know as Hitsville USA, wedged in between a funeral parlour and a beauty parlour.

With spare cash always a big problem, Berry just about managed to to complete a good enough recording studio, coming up with the ingenious idea of keeping everything he wanted to do strictly in house, while other record companies went to the expense of hiring essential equipment and artists. This meant that artists and musicians would often find themselves not only working on their own material but helping out other artists with whatever they were working on, creating the idea of one happy creative family reaching for stardom and success. To be successful at that time, Gordy became a tough taskmaster, making absolutely sure that his budding artists were never going to be allowed to become bigger than Motown, a point he proved years later when he allowed his number one star, Marvin Gaye, to leave the label to do his own thing.

He instilled in all his budding artists the knowledge that if they really wanted to succeed, then they were going to have to be "more than them white folks be", which was something that didn't fit too comfortably with some of his artists, accusing Berry of selling out to the whites; in which case they were promptly shown the door, to return to a life of low paid drudgery, dreaming of what could have been if they had just toed the line and accepted Berry's rule. Those who stayed were put through a thorough boot camp style education. Most of them were illiterate, extremely poor young people, unable to read and write, with few clothes to their name, but their voices more than made up for their inadequacies. They were taught how to read and write, how to use cutlery, how to speak polite and courteously, how to walk properly and how to conduct themselves in public, as well as being given beauty and deportment lessons. All along Berry insisted his artists looked and sounded nothing less than immaculate, glamorous ambassadors for his Motown label and to do this, he called in the services of a very special lady called Maxine Powell, who was given the task of transforming the young fledgling artists into confident superstars - and she did an admirable job of things, according to Diana Ross, who once said "Miss Powell taught me everything I know."

Maxine moved to Detroit in 1945, where she bought a large house that she called The Maxine Powell Finishing And Modelling School, which groomed the new stars to perfection. She said, "I teach class and class will always turn the heads of Kings and Queens backed up with determination and self belief." She was a lady who oozed glamour and style, and her regular Detroit fashion shows soon attracted the city's wealthiest people. At one show she met Berry Gordy, the two of them going on to share a fruitful and long lasting friendship that eventually saw Maxine accepting Berry's offer to come and work in Motown, where she was personally responsible for the development of the company's artists. Maxine Powell enjoyed a long, active life, passing away at the grand old age of ninety-one.

Prior to the time before the music of Tamla Motown became popular, all black music was bagged together under the offensive name of 'race music', to warn all good-living, God-fearing, respectable white folks to stay well clear. Berry was painfully aware of this, so he strived to produce music that the white folks not only accepted but loved. Once the appearances of the elegant Motown stars gathered momentum, Berry tailored his music to fit the change of opinion. Along with great images, he produced great, danceable music, which to some extent was neither white or black but oozed an irresistible magic that appealed to everyone who listened. The artists had to look better than the music, which again was down to the tutelage of Maxine Powell. The artists were part of a carefully conceived, nationwide advertising campaign containing the message that the new African American music was here to stay; and in return America started to fall in love with the distinct Tamla Motown sound Berry Gordy and his devoted team had worked tirelessly for years to perfect.

Ten bloody years had slipped by since America entered the Vietnam War and the army seemed no closer to their original objectives than they were when they first arrived. As increasing numbers of body bags were arriving home, the American public were having serious concerns about fighting a war many thought they were never going to win. Those soldiers who made it home in one piece, fully expecting a hero's return, were greeted by jeering crowds mocking them for taking part in a war America had nothing to do with. In the Second World War, American GIs proved themselves to be courageous soldiers but the big difference between that war and the one in Vietnam was that then they could see the enemy they were fighting, Germans and Japanese. In Vietnam, for most of the time, spotting the Vietnamese soldiers was nigh on impossible, like fighting an invisible enemy you knew were there but you couldn't see.

The GIs had to cope with fighting in a tough environment of dense impenetrable jungle and swamps infested with highly venomous snakes and spiders, and the psychological impact of having to do that every day must have shattered their morale. They were told by their superiors prior to leaving for 'Nam that the enemy they would encounter were no match for the Americans, merely a badly equipped, untrained peasant army made up of labourers and farmers. Nothing could have been further from the truth. They were indeed well trained, physically and mentally, fiercely patriotic and experts in jungle warfare; after all, it was their jungle. Plus they were absolute masters of the art of camouflage and concealment. American patrols would go out on missions unaware that only a few feet away the Vietcong were watching their every move. So sharp was their sense of smell, they could smell the Americans distances away, soaked in aftershave and chewing their spearmint gum.

Another terrifying nightmare the GIs had to face every time they ventured out on patrol was the very real danger of booby traps, which the Vietcong took to a whole new level. One commonly used booby trap was to dig a deep hole and fill it with punji sticks, razor sharpened bamboo sticks covered in faeces and urine. The whole trap was covered over with a criss cross of bamboo sticks, covered in leaves and foliage, making the trap undetectable to the GIs. The unfortunate victim would fall into the hole and be speared by the sharp bamboo sticks, causing wounds to go septic in no time at all. The Vietcong also used venomous snakes to their advantage, attaching them to the top of door frames. When the American patrol entered the village, any unsuspecting GI opening the door would be bitten by an extremely angry cobra or viper. The GIs had a phrase for snake bite victims: "one two three back" which was how long you had left to live before the venom killed you. Another lethal boobytrap was the mace, a heavy ball covered in punji sticks suspended high in the trees. All a GI had to do was to trigger the hidden trip wire and the ball would crash down in seconds, leaving the GI dead after being speared multiple times - dying an agonising death.

The Vietnam Peace Movement was gaining rapid support, giving rise to quite a few protest songs. Drug abuse among the troops was high, with top quality cocaine, heroin and marijuana as cheap as they come. Official figures point to over thirty percent of men using marijuana and ten percent using high grade heroin and coke. Fragging incidents were common: the deliberate killing of an officer ordering his men to go where they didn't want to go by using a fragmentation grenade. Patrols would purposely radio in false coordinates to company headquarters to avoid all contact with the Vietcong. Black GIs stuck together in little huts, listening to jazz, soul and funk, while white GIs listened to rock and country music from their huts. Soldiers were growing their hair long, with beards, and anti war slogans painted on their helmets and combat jackets. Discipline and morale was at an all-time low with rising instances of crime and disobedience. The eminent historian Shelby Stanton wrote "In the last years of the Army's retreat, its remaining forces were relegated to static security. Its decline was clearly apparent. Racial incidents, drug abuse, combat disobedience and crime reflected the growing idleness, resentment and frustration, the fatal handicap of a faulty campaign strategy was an incomplete waste of time and the tardy superficial attempts at Vietnamization." An entire American army was sacrificed on the battle for Vietnam. In America's twenty year involvement in the Vietnam war, fifty-eight thousand Americans were killed, of which forty-seven thousand four hundred and thirty-four were killed in combat with an additional three hundred and three thousand six hundred and forty-four wounded. The US destroyed over twenty percent of South Vietnam's jungles and between twenty to fifty percent of its forests and mangrove swamps with twenty-five million extremely toxic chemical herbicides.

In times of armed conflicts the world at large knows little about, it falls to the brave, unarmed war correspondents and journalists to record the action occurring in front of them, but often they miss the full picture. Take, for example, April 29th 1973 and the fall of Saigon to the Vietnamese army, rapidly advancing towards the beleaguered American embassy, where thousands of people had gathered hoping to be rescued. The embassy diplomats set themselves an impossible task of working hard to issue visas and other important documents the people would need to enter the States as helicopters landed and took off from the embassy grounds, carrying as many people as they could get aboard, but time was running out uncomfortably fast for the people stuck in the queues waiting to leave. Those of us old enough to remember watched in horror the last American helicopter lifting off from the roof of the embassy, people desperately clinging on to the skis until they could hold on no longer.

Meanwhile, behind those tragic scenes, a full US naval battle fleet was anchored offshore, waiting to go into action under the codename Operation Frequent Wind. Between the 29th and 30th of April, the US pilots ran an exhausting shuttle service from the mainland to the ships, many flying for over nineteen hours solid, landing, refuelling and taking off time and time again. Any spare helicopters taking up space on the carrier flight decks were simply thrown into the ocean to make valuable space. By the time the operation had ended, the American pilots had managed to rescue over ten thousand people, a fantastic achievement considering the time scale they had to work with. The real human tragedy to the day were the hundreds of personal files of all the people who had worked with the Americans who were left behind to face an uncertain future at the hands of the victorious Vietnamese army, facing long, harsh prison sentences or a summary execution. Months later, over one hundred and thirty-thousand Vietnamese people were repatriated in America, safe and ready to face a new life.

FIVE

My very earliest memories of Soho were driving up to London with my parents to spend days shopping and sightseeing, invariably ending up in Soho, which for me was an exciting, edgy neon labyrinth of different, alternative people. A curious assortment of gangsters, musicians and gentlemen of the road mixed with sexy ladies of the night, clustered together with their big hair, glossy crimson lips, accentuated eyes, tight dresses, stiletto heels and seamed stockings pointing the way for the excited onlooker, striking up a reasonable deal with their pimp and hoping to afford to spend some time in their garden of immeasurable pleasure, not to mention the frequent wealthy Tory peer idling past the queue of pretty rent boys in his Bentley looking for some fresh young flesh to spend the night with.

Quite often we'd end up in Meard Street, home to one of the craziest coffee houses I've ever been in: a downstairs basement called Le Macabre that had been going since the eighteenth century, where we'd sit and enjoy some great coffee on mock coffins, weird music playing in the background, black walls covered in plastic skeletons and pictures of a risqué nature depicting naked women wrapped around ghoulish creatures. Mum and Dad would sit there calmly flicking their cigarette ash into lifelike skulls, one of which I still have to this day, inscribed with the words Le Macabre and bringing back so many wonderful memories, every time I stare into its eyes, of a fabulous Soho at play, which is now being cleansed of all its vices and eccentricities which contributed big time in keeping it the unique Bohemian neon playground it once was, now a victim of the government's plan called gentrification.

One very special coffee bar, which stood on Old Compton Street, was called the 2ii's, a reference to the two

Iranian brothers who seized the opportunity for building up a prosperous business, which they did admirably so from 1956 up until 1970. The 2ii's wasn't just a coffee house, it also became the headquarters of the rock and roll scene, as the commemorative plaque on the wall of the original building, which is now a restaurant, proclaims:" The birthplace of British rock and roll and the popular music industry." For a time, when rock and roll was popular, before it lost out to the new blues and rhythm and blues music sweeping across the country, any talented, young, optimistic artist dreaming of being spotted by one of the talent scouts searching for fresh young talent would head for the 2ii's to try their luck. Two youngsters in particular owe everything they ever had to their early appearances in the 2ii's, Thomas Hicke and Harry Webb, who went on to international fame and fortune as Tommy Steele and Cliff Richard.

When I moved down to live and work in Brighton in the early nineties, I'd religiously spend two weekends a month reconnecting with the Soho I remembered as a child, drifting around some of the great pubs, some of which had been there for over a hundred years. The Coach and Horses, the Argyll Arms, the French House, The Dog and Duck for its delicious food, Jack Solomons and many others. They were interesting places packed with great characters, and I'd sit there, losing myself in the infectious Soho vibe, before wandering around the streets doing a spot of window shopping or buying a few sounds to add to my vinyl collection before taking the train back to Brighton.

There was the Arts Theatre Club once owned by those two lovable East End psychopaths Ronnie and Reg Kray, who entertained a host of glittering stars from Judy Garland, who the twins had a big soft spot for back in the day, to Old Blue Eyes. Paul Raymond's Revue Bar was a big slice of Soho history and entertainment since it first opened its doors back in 1958 on the site of the former Doric ballroom. At the time it was nigh on impossible for such a outrageous club to be allowed to feature nudes performing in public but Paul Raymond was one step ahead of the law by making the Revue Bar a private members only club. As people's tastes changed over time, the Revue Bar began to lose its popularity and was eventually forced to go into liquidation, closing in 2004. Paul Raymond's burlesque empire was done and dusted thanks to the onslaught of new entertainment tastes, though it resurfaced with a brand new, totally revamped show with the new name of the Soho Revue Bar; but that failed to stand the test of time and closed in January 2009, as one of Soho's landmarks became nothing more than just a cherished memory - gone, but I suspect never ever forgotten.

Sadly, today much of what made Soho the fabulous, diverse place it was is on the verge of gradually being swallowed up by the government's ridiculous plan called gentrification. These idiotic bureaucrats are intent on forcing what they perceive to be the perfect ultra-clean London on the population without having a clue that by destroying the past, the very things tourists from all over the world in their thousands want to see when they visit London will be lost. They will lose millions in tourist revenue each year. When will all this stupidity end? Sell off the Tower Bridge, the Tower of London, the Serpentine and the zoo, the museums and art galleries to multi-millionaire landlords desperate to fill their pockets with even more cash at London's expense. These changes have already begun, with the once famous Marquee club gone as well as the original Ronnie Scott's jazz club, which now serves expensive food in between the occasional saxophone riff as it clings on to its glorious past history.

The old Soho always dared to be that much more different than the rest of the London boroughs and a home for all kinds of people from different countries, where they felt safe no matter what their persuasion was. Increasingly high rents and gentrification have to a large extent destroyed

Soho's charm, making sure it fits in with everywhere else in London. Regrettably, it looks like it is going to end up a place where families will live happily ever after, bringing their children up in a safe, secure, antiseptic environment, a place where people go shopping and dine out in a modern expensive bistro discussing how much they enjoyed the latest West End show before the eleven o'clock last orders are called, signalling to all those who loved to stay out for the night soaking up the infectious Soho vibe to finish off their drinks and go home to bed. It's an insidious, unacceptable ethnic cleansing of everything that was good, dodgy, sexy, dangerous, dark, hedonistic and irresistible that was once the old Soho at night, caught in the neon glare, warts and all.

There is another, altogether more ruthless and frightening aspect going on: this new soulless Soho, many say, was the cause responsible for the sudden death of one of its greatest, most flamboyant characters one could ever wish to meet. He was a gay man called Bernie Katz, who was the gracious front of house manager of the famous Groucho Club, founded by Stephen Fry in 1985, intending it to become a haven of relaxation and conversation for artists and celebrities desperate to spend some quality time with like minded people far from the madding crowd. Princess Diana once enjoyed lunch there and Bill Clinton entertained the members with his saxophone. Patsy Kensit - who once famously battled with Liam Gallagher before he was banned - Sadie Frost, Noel Fielding, Sienna Miller, Melvyn Bragg, Damian Hurst and many other famous people were all members. Hurst, one night, so the story goes, dumped twenty thousand pounds behind the bar for everyone to enjoy his Turner Prize cash award for slicing a shark in half, while Bernie Katz's claim to fame occurred the night he ordered Madonna to leave the premises for using lewd language unbecoming to a woman, no matter how successful.

As gay as they come and completely unafraid to hide the fact, Bernie worked extremely hard to make the Groucho Club the place it was, devoting over twenty years of his life to welcoming in the members and making them feel special. He was the first port of call people would have to deal with, looking resplendent in his leopard print clothes and Cuban heels, but little did any of the clientele realise that Bernie's life fell apart shortly after he stopped working there. He quickly spiralled into debt as a result of his lifelong battle with the demon cocaine, running up a debt reputed to have been around thirty thousand pounds owed to the Albanian drug dealers who'd moved into Soho, ruling their clients with an unyielding iron fist.

There was a time when the drug trade was controlled by the Maltese and the Italians, who were much more lenient to clients who were having a bad time paying their debts back. More often than not they would have had a beating or two, maybe a little finger chopped off to remind them to never borrow if you can't pay back, but the Albanians are made of much crueller, violent stuff. When they lend out their cash they expect to be paid on time or face the consequences, showing absolutely zero leniency or understanding of their client's financial problems, which for Bernie proved fatal. His landlord found him hanging in his flat with not the slightest clue or evidence to ascertain if Bernie had been murdered or committed suicide. Some people attribute Bernie's unexpected death to his own theatrical way of showing the world that he was no longer willing to continue existing in the new Soho. Most of the people who knew him well shared a strong idea that Bernie was murdered by the Albanians, which leaves me wondering just what Ronnie and Reg would have had to say about one of their own being murdered. Affectionately known by one and all as the Prince of Soho, Bernie Katz was given a truly spectacular funeral with full military honours, the traditional horse-drawn East End hearse draped in flowers spelling out the Prince of Soho, a fitting tribute to a true old school Soho character loved by everyone.

I have vivid memories of arriving home after a long, sweaty, exhausting, amphetamine fuelled Wigan Casino soul night. As the last strains of the immortal three before eight faded and the early morning sunlight filtered through the old stained glass window, after handshakes, hugs and earnest promises of meeting up next week, we picked up our bags and headed for the exit for the long journey home. Some people driving offered lifts to those in need, and the less fortunate walked up to the station to spend a couple of hours huddled together on the waiting room floor, hands cupped around hot chocolate or a cold can of cider depending on the time of year, dreaming of getting home and jumping in the bath, hoping to soak away another amphetamine downer. All part and parcel of being a regular on the endlessly demanding northern soul scene.

Crashed out on the bed in my tiny upstairs bedroom, eyes wide open, heart pounding, facing another bleak week on the building site was a nightmare to say the least. Background music was anything but soul music, something much less frenetic to chill me out. Maybe some early Rod Stewart or Stones or the Genesis album *Trick of the Tail* or the jazz classic *So What* by Miles Davis, which is still one my favourite albums, eyes closed, crashed out on the bed with a mug of creamy Horlicks before drifting off into a deep coma-like sleep.

More often than not just lying there in the darkness, I enjoyed listening to the man whose gravel-like voice reminded me of a gruff Coleman Hawkins saxophone solo and the man who did more than most in establishing a vibrant, fresh British blues scene as a force to be reckoned with and then some… I am of course talking about the late, great, singularly unique Alexis Korner, whose Sunday night radio show, Alexis Korner's Blues and Soul Show, I rarely missed on my journeys back down to reality. Alexis was born in Paris in April 1928, where he lived with his parents before moving to London to escape the Nazi persecution. Throughout the 50s and 60s, traditional jazz - trad jazz - was to be heard just about everywhere in Britain before the invasion of rock and roll, played by musicians who added their own take on the music that had originally come out of New Orleans, including the likes of Chris Barber, Kenny Ball, Humphrey Littleton, the one and only Acker Bilk, George Chisum and Terry Lightfoot.

Arguably the most popular artist at the time was Acker Bilk, who regularly appeared on various television shows. I can just about remember watching him on the box with his goatee beard, striped waistcoat and black bowler hat, a truly larger than life character who really did champion trad jazz, which to most young people at the time sounded far too old-fashioned and conservative. Despite the gradual decline, Acker Bilk scored a massive worldwide instrumental hit with the song most of us who were around at the time can still remember. The instantly recognisable 'Stranger on the Shore' featured him playing the clarinet at its smoothest sound ever, earning the song more than fifty weeks in the charts, reaching number two, as well as number one in the American Billboard Hot 100 chart together with a gold disc for selling over one million copies worldwide. Acker was without doubt the hottest trad jazz artist of his time, going on to star in two motion pictures, awarded the MBE for services rendered and the BBC's prestigious Gold Jazz Award. Had it not been for the rock and roll invasion, doubtless Acker would have gone on to enjoy so much more success, but the times were most definitely changing and how. Despite his fall from favour, he continued enjoying his musical career for many years before he succumbed to bladder cancer and a stroke, the man who once described 'Stranger on the Shore' as his old age pension fund.

Ironically enough, Alexis Korner, who became a truly great blues artist, started out as a member of Chris

Barber's jazz band, but he soon began his mission to alter the course of music after meeting a brilliant blues harmonica player called Cyril Davies, who readily joined Alexis in his crusade to change the London music scene. They quickly set to work creating the legendary Blues and Barrelhouse club in Soho on the corner of Wardour and Brewer Street, which originally was a skiffle music venue. Thanks to a number of Chris Barber's American music contacts, the club attracted some big names including Sister Rosetta Stone, Brother John Sellers, Champion Jack Dupree, Otis Span and the great Muddy Waters who was the first artist to appear in the club to play an electric guitar, creating a unique sound that instantly convinced both Alexis and Cyril that loud amplified music was definitely the way forward.

In March 1962 the duo moved from Soho to Ealing Jazz Club on the Broadway, a venue that was managed by the talented, sharply dressed Fery Asgari, who was putting on two jazz nights a week with a Saturday strictly blues night. The impressive list of budding artists who were eventually to become music legends who flocked to the club included Eric Clapton, Rod Stewart, Ginger Baker, Jack Bruce, Long John Baldry, Paul Jones, Manfred Man, Eric Burden, John McLaughlin and mod legends-to-be The Who - or The Detours as they were known back then - who played in the club when they were starting out. The club was also famous for bringing the Rolling Stones together after Alexis is reputed to have introduced Mick Jagger and Keith Richards to Brian Jones and Charlie Watts, and as we all know the rest is legendary rock and roll history.

The blues scene was on the verge of exploding in London, so much so that the club attracted the owner of The Marquee club, Harry Pendleton, who insisted on wanting to take a look for himself at what was going on, to see what was so special that Alexis and Cyril were creating. He was impressed by what he saw and offered Alexis a regular Thursday night spot in The Marquee after the club had hit some financially troubled waters after switching from playing jazz to rhythm and blues. The new policy worked better than Harry could have ever imagined, the place packed to the rafters, with a number of reports at the time claiming that the blues nights were attended by over five hundred people who came to dance the night away to the new infectious blues sound. The 100 Club in Oxford Street was also soon doing a roaring trade after switching from jazz to blues, so much so that it managed to attract a number of big names including Sister Rosetta Tharpe and the legendary Howlin Wolf, as well as two fairly established British bands, The Atwoods and The Kinks.

In addition to becoming a major force on the blues scene, Alexis Korner also enjoyed a hugely successful broadcasting career, interviewing many showbiz celebrities as well as writing articles for various newspapers and magazines, in addition presenting his brilliant Sunday night jazz and blues show that ran for many years. A fresh approach to music saw him team up with Peter Thorup in creating the brilliant Collective Consciousness Society, CCS for short, enjoying a number of hit singles that Mickie Most had a big say in producing. This talented pioneer of the new blues music scene died of cancer at the young age of fifty-five years in January 1984, leaving us all with a rich artistic legacy still popular today in the right circles. The one and only Alexis Korner, the musician hailed as the founding father of the British blues music scene.

The Ealing Jazz Club is still there, having seen many changes over the decades. The club responsible for giving birth to the blues includes a casino and a disco and has boasted many name changes but now operates under the name The Red Room and is still a live music venue. The original club is still remembered thanks to a commemorative plaque proclaiming "The Ealing Jazz Club March 7th 1962 where Alexis Korner and Cyril Davis began British rhythm and blues on this site." As a result, there is a wonderful, nostalgic film documentary called *Suburban Steps To Rockland* that takes an in depth look at the history of the club and the many artists that played there and features interviews with Paul Jones, John Mayall, Don Craine, Eric Burden Terry Marshall and Dick Taylor. If you are into the early days of the birth of the blues, it's a film most definitely not to be missed.

But in Soho back then, the music scene wasn't just about trad jazz and blues. There was a plethora of cool nightclubs playing all kinds of music from around the world. There was the Caribbean Club, the Contemporanean in Mayfair, Club 59, Club 77, Havaga Greek Club, the Count Sickle Cue Club, the Last Chance Club, the 100 Club, the Bag O' Nails, the Scene, the Flamingo and the Club Americano to name but a few in the constantly changing musical landscape. From the pictures I've studied and the research done, the two clubs I would have loved to have experienced were the Club Americano and the Flamingo, both of which were located in the basement of the Mapleton Hotel on Coventry Street, a magnificent old building sadly no longer there due to it being converted into a more modern hotel.

So the legend goes, Billy Fury, who was making a name for himself at the time, sacked off his backing band because they were getting a bit to jazzy for his liking. Talk about a big mistake - because the band just happened to be Georgie Fame and the Blue Flames, who signed up for a three year residency in the Flamingo. Tony Harris, who was the manager of the Mapleton Hotel, met a jazz fan and pianist named Jeffrey Kruger and discussed how he wanted to change the face of jazz into a much more socially acceptable scene and do away with the dark, sleazy, smoke filled joints normally associated with the jazz scene. It seemed an impossible task to pull off but Kruger decided to give it a go and in August 1962 he staged an opening night in the hotel called Jazz At The Mapleton.

The club soon started to attract the likes of Ronnie Scott, Johnny Dankworth, and Kenny Graham's Afro Cubists. Kruger fell in love with one particular song of theirs so much that he renamed the club Flamingo and the legend was born. It was a tight squeeze going downstairs and into the small club, where you were told that the place operated a strict no alcohol policy but you could help yourself to as many soft drinks as possible. The club was soon acquiring a great reputation as the place to be if you wanted to listen to quality musicians and this gave Kruger the confidence to pull off the impossible by convincing the one and only Billie Holiday to come and sing at the Flamingo after finishing her concert at the Albert Hall the same night.

Billie turned up late, looking absolutely drop dead gorgeous in a full length gold gown, and performed 'Willow Weep For Me' and 'Lover Man'. She completely intimidated tenor saxophonist Ronnie Scott to the point where he felt he couldn't play a note just watching her perform in the flesh; and who wouldn't be intimidated by such an acclaimed artist? According to one witness, Billie felt so at home in the club that she went on to sing several songs before bidding the mesmerised audience goodnight and vanishing. Other big names who appeared at the Flamingo included Mary Lou Williams, Dick Lee, Sarah Vaughn, Billy Daniels, Joe Harriott, Tubby Hayes, Stevie Wonder, Bill Haley, Patti Labelle, Dizzy Gillespie, The Animals, The Stones, The Moody Blues, Eric Clapton, Cream, Alexis Korner, Ginger Baker, Jack Bruce and the one and only Ella Fitzgerald, earning the Flamingo the accolade of being Britain's finest modern jazz club. John Mayall once described the Flamingo as "a very dark and evil smelling basement. It had that seedy sort of atmosphere and there was a lot of pill popping. You usually had to scrape people up off the floor when you emerged into Soho at dawn." It's a description that wasn't that far away from the scene going on in the Catacombs, the Golden Torch, the

Twisted Wheel, Blackpool Mecca and Wigan Casino. In fact the similarities we later shared on the northern soul scene with the original mods are striking. We loved soul music, we loved dark, dirty, sweaty dives in which we danced the night away to soul music, and we loved amphetamines, the icing on the cake, keeping us bright eyed and bushy tailed from dusk till dawn. I still find it amazing that within a tight nucleus four London clubs in such a short distance of each other, the Flamingo, the 100 Club, the Bag O' Nails and the Scene in Ham Yard, were responsible for laying down the blueprint of the future northern soul scene that has lasted over sixty years and is still going as strong as ever, attracting younger people searching for something different they can be a part of away from mobile phones, laptops, Tik Tok, Twitter and Instagram, determined to make their own individual mark, dancing and making genuine friends the way we did, now the older statesmen of the scene.

And yet there was more to emerge from the cramped confines of the Mapleton Hotel, and if the many caught in the moody black and white photographs are anything to go by, the Club Americano was another of those places you just had to be seen in to sample the unique vibe of spending the night in Little America. Trendy, smart black guys, many of whom were US serviceman stationed in England, hair slicked back, in their loose, baggy double-breasted suits and colourful silk ties, dancing the night away with gorgeous girls with big hair, immaculate make up and tight dresses. For the princely sum of ten shillings, you were served a three course meal of tomato soup, chicken and chips and a bowl of ice cream while listening to the coolest jazz this side of the Atlantic.

The club boasted a mixed crowd during the time when outside Soho, the colour bar was still in operation in many pubs, clubs and dancehalls across the country. It was run by two popular brothers in and around Soho called Ricky and Johnny Gunnell, who eventually moved the club to

Wardour Street where they started the Saturday all-nighters. Sadly, due to a vicious knife fight occurring in the club between two former lovers of Christine Keeler, who was a frequent and extremely popular visitor to the club, more and more black Americans were banned, so they gradually went elsewhere, grooving the night away to the increasingly popular jazz and rhythm and blues played at the Flamingo, but what crazy, wild and wonderful stories about the Club Americano could be told if only a club could talk. Later on, the Gunnell brothers branched out into the music industry with a booking and management service, looking after the business affairs of many famous artists including Cliff Bennett, Fleetwood Mac, Slade, Rod Stewart, John Mayall and many others. In addition to that they opened up the Ram Jam club on Brixton High Street, where the legend himself, Mister Otis Redding, made his first ever British debut.

SIX

Before we head downstairs to the 100 Club, I talked to a number of people about the various clubs they liked and I had some surprisingly mixed responses when it came to the 100 Club. Some really enjoyed it and some didn't. I heard comments like the place is just too small and the toilets are a complete disaster. Well, the toilets in Wigan were equally disgusting, so no valid arguments on that topic for sure. Some based their arguments on that old tiresome misbelief that the 100 Club didn't play proper northern soul but played more modern stuff that didn't fit in with the outdated, fast, stomping, classic northern 60s sounds. I only visited the 100 Club on three occasions and I enjoyed what I heard. Yes, there were some modern records being played that I didn't recognise, alongside some classics that were big back in the day. For me, the contrasting sounds worked well; and let's not forget that modern soul only stays modern for a short time, that those records eventually turn into familiar classics in their own right. But you know the old saying: you can't please all of the people all of the time.

Later on, continuing the discussions with a number of people who were there back in the day, I asked some of them what they consider to be the greatest northern soul club ever. They responded with perfectly understandable viewpoints based on personal experiences. "The Catacombs was the best, mate – No way, the Torch was without a doubt the best – No way, the Twisted Wheel was – Sorry, Wigan Casino by far was the ultimate northern club going that ever was – Yeah but what about the Highland Room, that changed the scene round with the records they played up there." All pretty valid comments but in my opinion, only ever being a Wigan regular, and yes it was pretty awesome, it was no better than the rest. Different definitely; but not better. They were the main clubs that helped put northern soul on the map. The main deejays played in all of the clubs, and the records they played became popular in all the clubs, so to say one was better than the other is a viewpoint based purely on personal sentimentality. I like to look on them as part of one big happy northern soul family, out there enjoying themselves, doing what they did and continue to do best.

THE 100 CLUB OXFORD STREET – SOHO – 1942 – PRESENT DAY

Looking up at the sign proclaiming the 100 Club, it's impossible to put a price on the immense contribution to the music industry, both here and in America, it has made over the decades. The club came to prominence way back in 1942 when it was first a restaurant featuring one night a week jazz sessions. These nights quickly became popular in a short space of time and it was called the Feldman Swing Club featuring an in house band: saxophonists Jimmy Skidmore and Frank Weir, Kenny Baker on trumpet, and a ridiculously young Victor Feldman on drums. As the word spread rapidly that the club was the place to be if you were into authentic jazz bebop and swing, it attracted a large, cool clientele of black American GIs adding their own unique individuality and style to the place by dancing the jitterbug, strangely enough a style of dance that was banned in a number of London clubs at the time. On any given night there was a good chance that you would be rubbing shoulders with celebrities like Glenn Miller, Mel Powell, Benny Goodman, Art Pepper, Roy McKinley, Johnny Dankworth, Ronnie Scott, Lee Konitz, Archie Shepp, and Sonny Stitt together with black musicians Frank Holder from Guyana, Jamaican-born George Goode and Ray Ellington.

Then in the early 60s, with the emergence of the rhythm and blues music scene, the 100 Club soon became the place to be seen in if you happened to be a young, sharp, pill popping mod looking for some sexy chick to dance the night away with you. This continued for a number of years until the club took a massive change in musical direction in September 1976 when it became the unlikely host to the International Punk Rock Festival. The bands that appeared read like punk royalty: Buzzcocks, Sex Pistols, Dammed, Stranglers, UK Subs, Angelic Upstarts, Siouxsie and the Banshees and many more. Thankfully, and many would agree, the club underwent another new direction which in my opinion has made it one of the greatest northern soul clubs on the scene. On October 24th 1979 the club staged the very first northern soul all-nighter, which is still going just as strong today as it ever did.

The idea for the change was the brainchild of the one and only Mister Ady Croasdell, who needs absolutely no introduction if you are into the northern scene. He's a man who has dedicated his life and passion in championing black American soul music, making him in my opinion a true ambassador to the scene, working tirelessly to keep northern soul music alive alongside fellow deejays Randy Cozens RIP, Butch and many others who have made their mark in the place where it all began, back in the early 60s. Record collector, deejay, promoter, and the man behind the respected soul music record label Kent Records, Ady was born in Sheffield and his incredible journey into the northern soul scene is typical for many of us back in the day. For Ady, a lifelong love affair began in 1967, when he first heard northern soul being played in the Frollocking Knee Cap pub in Market Harborough. After finishing university, he started his working life selling vast quantities of northern soul singles in Rupert Street market in London. It was during this time, in 1974, that he took the life changing decision to become a record dealer, and just like many of the scene's deejays he headed for America in search of black gold, searching high and low for quality rare singles. Ady became a prominent mover and shaker on the London scene, along with his lifelong friend Randy Cozens, both of them spreading the northern soul gospel with the establishment of the grandly titled 60s Rhythm And Soul Society. Their reason for this was simple: they just wanted to listen to some quality soul music, and even today, much to his credit and with undying patience, Ady is still out there hunting for those elusive singles that have slipped through the net over the course of time.

Away from the 100 Club, Ady became the man behind the hugely successful Cleethorpes northern soul events, in a place he loved so much as a child, spending holidays in the holiday camp with his family. From shaky beginnings, the Cleethorpes all-nighter was a success thanks to Ady going out on a limb to book so many of the northern soul artists we used to listen to: Doris Troy, Hoagy Lands, Spencer Wiggins, Lou Courtney, Sydney Barnes, Little Carl Carlton, Betty Lavelle, Toby Lark, Bobby Hutton, Tommy Hunt, Al Wilson, the Velvelettes, Barbara Lewis and others. In my opinion, if there was a Grammy award for dedicating your life to the northern soul scene and so much more, then Ady Croasdell would win it hands down.

I've only done the 100 Club three times and I thoroughly enjoyed myself on each occasion, meeting new people on the scene who were the same as me only distances apart. I spoke to Ady a couple of times and found him to be an easy, friendly, knowledgeable, approachable guy, just like I hoped he would be. Before the all-nighter I remember hanging about outside asking myself do I really want to do this, descending the stairs with some trepidation akin to venturing into the unknown, surrounded by a strong sense of history and thinking about the number of artists who went before me up and down the stairs. Dark, aged walls with some graffiti of the names of past northern soul clubs. Most definitely the smallest northern venue I've been in, with a small stage area and two or three record dealers sitting at tables selling sounds. I grabbed a pint and moved away from the dancefloor, noticing some exceptional dancers going through their moves so effortlessly, moves that I could never pull off even in my prime, so for me it was a night hiding in the shadows talking to people here and there about their own experiences on the northern scene.

Photographer and film director Elaine Constantine, who made that brilliant film called *A Northern Soul*, gives a brilliant insight to the 100 Club as follows:" I often spot a first timer entering the doorway that brings you immediately back onto a dark and packed out dancefloor. It's like watching yourself entering all over again for the first time. You'll see people trying desperately to recognise some music, barely in before they're faced with a kaleidoscope of sweat covered faces that emerge and retreat quickly through weak sporadic shades of light. It's impossible to stay dry or stand still. Will I remain intact?

"My first time, I was working for the *Face* magazine in the 90s. There was an assignment, not a night out. I thought I could just go in there, get some good photography then leave, a one off visit. I had left the all night scene back in the 80s since becoming a photographer and moving to London. I know now that when I entered, it must have been Butch or Ady playing as I didn't recognise at least half of the records they were playing but they sounded good. New discoveries great to hear and that sheer enthusiasm that I thought had gone away since I stopped going to those things up north was there again. That was a lovely thing to hear after years away and especially experiencing other types of clubs. I thought fair enough so I stopped for a while and sat on the edge of the stage taking it all in and trying to work it out. I had enough images in my camera or should I try for more. I'm not really sure what happened next but a track came on that I knew - 'You Left Me' - The Vibrations. I got up and my legs were moving around before I'd even had the chance to think that I wasn't an observer anymore. I was a partaker. I still don't know what happened that night to make a difference but I knew I'd found a second home. Maybe it was Ady's music policy coupled with the fact it's just so bloody dark. It was all these diehards with the opportunity to simply dance to the music without being on show which is quite liberating especially since the arrival of social media. I know there's nowhere else quite like it. It keeps me coming back for more. I met my husband on the dancefloor and many close friends so it's not going to be easy to get away from now even if I wanted to."

That night I stayed the course from dusk until dawn, chatting to many people with identical interests and enjoying the music, which was a cool mix of the old and the new that blended well. I left the 100 Club fully convinced that it was a great northern soul club playing underground music in a dingy, cramped, sweaty space tucked well below the Soho streets. A secret hideaway from the hustle and bustle of everyday normal life for one night - but better that than nothing at all. I really hope that the 100 Club remains one of London's alternate landmarks, protected from the greedy hands of multi-million pound property developers who see no good whatsoever in the past. And there they are, carrying out that senseless policy of gentrification without realising they are demolishing the invaluable old landmarks of London that make it one of the truly great cities in which to live and visit, and long may it continue doing that for all our sakes.

At the end of my third and last 100 Club all-nighter I managed to behave myself throughout the night, turning down offers of pills and powders, sticking to a few lagers instead, leaving me feeling like some refreshment before catching the train back to Brighton. Seeing that I was in the area and not having visited the Bar Italia for ages, that's where I headed for. I had a bad thought that it might have fallen victim to the developers but thankfully not a chance, and it felt great seeing it again having kept the original vibe that's made the place the spiritual hang out for mods and Soho's colourful bohemia. It was opened in 1949 by Italian husband and wife Louigi and Caterina Polledi, who met and fell in love in London. Surely they could not have had the slightest idea how special the Bar Italia would become in rapidly changing London. Would you believe the original Gaggia coffee machine is still there on the counter, operating as smooth as silk from the first day it was installed over forty years ago; and how many thousands of cups of coffee has it got through since then? The colourful decor on the walls is untouched and the fabulous mosaic tiled floor is once again as good as the day it was laid by their grandfather and a lasting tribute to traditional craftsmanship of a time gone by. I sat outside enjoying the early morning sun with a bacon and egg ciabatta, with a glass of malt whisky and a chilled Peroni for good measure, revelling in the feeling that no change is absolutely the best change. I sincerely hope that the Bar Italia resists the ridiculous development plans that claimed the Marquee and Ronnie Scott's jazz club, which reminds me: I'm going to have pay another visit before too long. Long live the Bar Italia.

THE FLAMINGO CLUB – WARDOUR STREET –
SOHO 1952 – 1969

A quote from back in the day not only described the Flamingo club perfectly but also a number of run down clubs on the northern soul scene: "from the narrow dimly lit neon entrance, you entered a sleazy subterranean den of style and iniquity. Intoxicating and the people stayed there until sunrise." These words describe just what the northern soul clubs were like, apart from the Highland Room. We loved dancing, we loved soul music, we loved dirty, dark, sweaty dives and we loved amphetamines to keep us all bright eyed and bushy tailed from dusk till dawn. The Flamingo was one of the four clubs that played a big part in the early London rhythm and blues scene. Originally it was a jazz club before the music policy changed to blues music. The dingy decor attracted a whole world of dubious people, gangsters, pimps, West Indians, queers and prostitutes trying their best to grab as much cash as they could from the wealthy US servicemen who frequented the club on a regular basis.

The club's name came from a song called 'Flamingo' that was first recorded back in 1940 by the Duke Ellington Orchestra, released on Victor Records and later adopted as the club's signature tune. The club was managed by two brothers, Rik and Johnny Gunnel, well known doormen and wannabe entrepreneurs who later owned their own club on the Brixton Road called The Ram Jam in honour of their musical hero Geno Washington, who frequently played there. Throughout the 1950s the Flamingo attracted quite a lot of established successful artists including Sarah Vaughn and Billie Holliday along with respected blues musicians Long John Baldry, Eric Clapton, John Mayall, the Moody Blues, Alexis Korner, The Animals, Georgie Fame and Rod Stewart. American artists who played there included Bill Haley, Stevie Wonder, John Lee Hooker, Patty Labelle, Dizzy Gillespie, Otis Redding, Wilson Pickett and Geno Washington. Other big names who appeared there were Mary Lou Williams, Dick Lee, Billy Daniels, Joe Harriott, Tubby Hayes, Stevie Wonder, Ginger Baker, Jack Bruce and the one and only Ella Fitzgerald, who gave it the accolade of being Britain's finest modern jazz club.

In 1963, with the Flamingo reported to be the coolest club to hang out in, large numbers of mods used it and as more and more people filled the club each night, English songwriter, record producer and musician Ralph Samwell actually recorded a live album called *Blues At The Flamingo* featuring Georgie Fame and the Blue Flames, who acquired a three year residency in the club. I've heard the album a number of times and to be fair, it really does capture the hot, sweaty, chattering atmosphere of a night in the Flamingo. The club was also one of the earliest venues to regularly feature West Indian ska music, going some way in breaking down the colour barrier between white and black youths. One artist in particular who worked hard at promoting peace and unity between white and black audiences was a popular Jamaican sound engineer and artist called Wilbert Augustas, who was better known as Count Suckle. He popularised not only Jamaican reggae but also Afro Caribbean culture in the UK.

Wilbert originally worked in the insurance business but because he owned a substantial record collection of rhythm and blues and soul he put his hobby to good use by deejaying in the Scene club. In 1964 he started to run the ultra cool Sue record label, releasing a number of successful singles by Rufus Thomas, Ike and Tina Turner, Charlie and Inez Foxx, Elmore James, Wilbert Harrison and Donnie Elbert. He also managed to persuade Chuck Berry to come and play in Britain after he paid the bail money to get Chuck out of jail. He was the deejay for a time at the Roaring Twenties club in Carnaby Street but due to heavy police presence because of the drug scene, he moved to the Cue club in Praed Street, Paddington, where he became hugely popular and was reputed to be the first artist to include rap music in his repertoire. Of his time at the Cue club, he said: "We led the field because we were always moving with the times. When we opened ska was the big thing and the artists who played the Cue club included Prince Buster, Rico, Tommy McCook, Don Drummond and Roland Alfonso. They all played here when visiting London. We played all the latest things so new dances caught on quick." Wilbert Augustus Campbell AKA Count Suckle died in 2014, after a heart attack, depriving the scene of a truly great innovator of his time.

THE BAG O' NAILS CLUB – KINGLY STREET, SOHO
1965 – 1968

Originally the club became well established in the 1930s and put to good use during the London Blitz as an air raid shelter. During the 1960s it was run by the Gunnel brothers, who ran both the Flamingo and the Ram Jam clubs. On the 25th November 1966, the place was jam packed with an assortment of people who'd come to watch a one-off special performance by Jimi Hendrix. The audience included some prominent names in the music industry, including Jimmy Page, Jeff Beck, The Stones and Paul McCartney. The Bag O' Nails club differed from other clubs at the time because the regulars who used to hang out there didn't just go for the music policy. They simply enjoyed the cosy, relaxing, upmarket atmosphere, chilling out with each other. The club benefitted by having a drinks licence as well as serving food. News spread fast that Jimi Hendrix was in town to play, described in the following words:" When Jimi first came to England, Chas Chandler had put the word out that he'd found a phenomenal guitarist in New York and he could play the guitar behind his back and with his teeth. The buzz was out before Jimi had even been here so people were anticipating his performance and he more than lived up to what we were expecting."

Terry Reid, rock vocalist, commented:" We were all hanging out in the Bag O' Nails, Keith, Mick, Brian, Paul, Geff Beck and Jimmy Page. I thought what's this. A bloody convention or something. Then here comes Jimi in one of his military jackets, hair all over the place and he pulls out this left handed Fender Stratocaster beat to hell looking like he'd been chopping wood with it and then he gets up all soft spoken and all of a sudden – WHOOORRRAAZZ. And then he breaks into 'Wild Thing' and it was all over. There were guitar players weeping, they had to mop up the floor. He was piling it on solo after solo, I could see everyone's fillings falling out. When he finished it was silence. Nobody knew what to do, everybody was dumbstruck completely in shock."

Geff Beck commented:" The thing I noticed was not only his amazing blues but his physical amount on the guitar. His actions were all on one chord, an explosive package. Me, Eric and Jimmy were cursed because we were from Surrey. We all looked a bit like we'd walked out of Burtons mens shop window. He hit me like an earthquake when he arrived. I had to think long and hard about what I did next. For me the first shockwave was Jimi Hendrix. That was the major thing that shook everybody up. Even though we'd all been established ourselves as fairly safe in the guitar field, he came along and reset the rules in one evening. Most thing you know next, Eric moving along with Cream and it was kicking off in big chunks."

Mick Jagger commented:" I loved Jimi Hendrix from the beginning. The moment I saw him I thought he was fantastic. I was an instant convert. Mister Jimi Hendrix was the best thing I'd ever seen. It was exciting, sexy and interesting. He didn't have a very good voice but he made up for that with his guitar."

Pete Townshend commented: "The thing that really stunned me and Eric was the way he took what we did and made it better and I really started to play. I thought I'd never be as great as he was but there was certainly no reason why I shouldn't try. I remember saying to Eric I'm going to play him off the stage one day but what Eric said was even more peculiar. He said well I'm going to pretend that I'm Jimi Hendrix."

THE SCENE CLUB - GREAT WINDMILL STREET - SOHO 1963 - 1966

The Scene club was the hot spot everyone was talking about back then. It offered no comforts or luxuries for the clientele. All it consisted of was a large room with black walls and a deejay area. It was a club for serious mods wanting to dance the night away. As Pete Townshend said, it was "a place where we came to dance, to learn all the right moves." What the club lacked in comfort certainly made up for with the music policy, which was the responsibility of one man who was getting a big name for himself on the rhythm and blues scene. He was called Guy Stevens and he had all his fingers buried deep when it came down to knowing everything there was to know about rare, imported, Stateside rhythm and blues. He also worked as a record producer, as well as managing a number of bands including Mott the Hoople, Procul Harem and the mighty Clash, working with them closely on their classic album *London Calling*.

The club itself boasted quite an impressive history, rapidly becoming a cool hangout for all kinds of musicians going as far back as the 1930s. Around 1948 it became a jazz club, going under the appropriate name of The Downbeat Club and featuring its own in-house band of the same name. The club also hosted The Pinstripe Club, which became the favourite haunt of the good, the bad and the not so bad, where it is said Christine Keeler first met the wealthy Tory peer and minister for war John Profumo, leading to one of the biggest sex scandals of the decade, which so nearly brought the Conservative government to its knees and caused the unfortunate Mister Profumo to resign.

The club was run by a charismatic entrepreneur from Ireland called Ronan O' Rahilly, who harboured a strong rebellious nature throughout most of his life and was expelled from school seven times. He was the son of a man who was killed fighting for Ireland during the bloody Easter

Rising in 1916 in Dublin. He arrived in London at the age of seventeen and soon started frequenting places where the wealthy and creative people hung out. He jumped at the opportunity to run the Scene club in Great Windmill Street, where he quickly befriended Guy Stevens before throwing himself headlong into the music industry, booking Alexis Korner, the Stones, Zoot Money and Chris Farlowe to appear in the club as well as creating the first ever pirate radio station, Radio Caroline.

Meanwhile Guy Stevens had already developed a deep passion for rhythm and blues music, boasting a sizeable collection of original imported Stateside singles and LPs, and he convinced Ronan to let him have one night a week in the club playing these records; and so the former insurance broker was ready for action. The Scene rapidly became the coolest place to hang out in with deejay Guy on the decks playing the new music the kids just couldn't get enough of. As a nifty side line, Guy used to record his records on cassette tapes and bring them into the club to sell to the soul-starved kids. In 1964 his big chance came when Chris Blackwell of Island records offered him the job of running Sue Records, as well as bringing American artists over to play in England. Kids were going mad for the records Guy was playing from virtually unknown artists like Bobby Parker, Betty Everett, BB King, JB Lenoir, Willie Mabon, Elmore James, Donnie Elbert, Rufus Thomas, Inez and Charlie Foxx, Wilbert Harrison, and Ike and Tina Turner.

He was fast becoming the rhythm and blues guru who knew everything about the music, carrying his vast collection around in a wooden trunk. His unexpected downfall began when Keith Moon gave Guy his first taste of speed, and he loved it - and from that moment on, he was trapped in a downward spiral, taking more and more drugs and becoming an alcoholic. Following a number of drug offences, he was jailed for several months; and if that wasn't bad enough, he arrived home to discover that his entire record collection had been stolen - which drove him to have a complete nervous breakdown. Chris Blackwell stepped in again in an attempt to get Guy back in the driving seat where he belonged but the damage had been done.

It was such a tragic end to a man who'd given his all to the music industry and been a key figure in promoting and playing the music he loved forever. In 1981 he was found dead in his apartment after taking an overdose of drugs prescribed to him to help reduce his dependency on booze, dying at the age of only forty-one years old. Meanwhile Ronan O' Rahilly contracted vascular dementia, forcing him to return to Ireland, living in a private nursing home in County Louth where he died on the 20th April 2020 at the age of seventy-nine. RIP Mister Guy Stevens, a man ahead of his time.

That very early embryonic rhythm and blues scene was fast growing in popularity thanks to the early mods; and they looked the part. Noting had gone before to beat the their cool image, clustered around Soho, chatting away before heading down to one of the clubs for a sweaty amphetamine all-nighter. Their image then and now was unbeatable, an intoxicating mix of fine English tailoring and with touches of French and Italian style backed up with a discerning English street cred attitude. In some ways they became living, moving works of art whenever they were seen out and about on their Vespa and Lambretta scooters, some favouring a clean, bog standard factory look while others went the full way, their scooters festooned with chrome front and back crash bars, backrests, whip aerials with fox tails attached, Union Jack seats, whitewall tyres and flyscreens boasting custom paintwork or chrome plating making a highly personal statement whenever they were out and about in London or driving down to the coast for the weekend, leaving passers by gaping in astonishment; but they do say that beauty is in the eye of the beholder and for a mod, making a personal statement is everything.

In my opinion there is little that separates mods from northern soulies. The uniforms may be different but that apart, their hearts beat to the same rhythm with the same passion, love and energy. In the 100 Club, the Flamingo, the Bag O' Nails and the Scene, those early mods set down the foundations for the future northern soul scene still going as strong as ever sixty years later. Who could have possibly thought that a secretive alternative music scene courtesy of rare imported American soul music could have lasted that long; and then to top it all, did any of us possibly conceive that the northern soul scene would have been celebrated in the Royal Albert Hall on a fabulous night to remember featuring a selection of northern soul classic songs backed up with a full symphony orchestra? Just another incredible aspect of the Strange World Of Northern Soul.

SEVEN

And so it's now time to wish Soho a heartfelt farewell and good luck as we head north, beginning with the man who more than anybody else at the time championed and promoted American soul music. There is a beautiful quote from a songwriter by the name of Micheal Somerset who summed up just how much respect the northern soul people had for this man and it goes like this:" I went to a Northern Soul reunion with Dave back in the early 90s and I gave him a suit made from a heavyweight dark rich grey material called Thornproof cut in a Victorian style. For some reason I had two made so I gave one to Dave as a gift. He loved it, it fitted him like a glove and he looked amazing so there I was in this soul club and there were a lot of leading lights on the Northern Soul scene in and suddenly there was a hush in the room as Dave walked in looking immaculate in the suit and it was almost like a meeting of vampires and Dracula had just turned up." I'm talking about the one and only Mister Dave Godin, a seemingly ordinary, unobtrusive guy who was anything but when it came to the subject of soul music. A guy I met and shook hands with ever so briefly when he turned up at Wigan Casino to check out the scene he'd been hearing so much about in readiness for a feature he was writing for *Blues and Soul* magazine, in which he later recalled that he really enjoyed himself.

There is a charming little story of how he actually discovered the music he fell in love with forever that makes for amusing reading. Dave the young teenager from Bexley Heath was literally seconds away from his life-changing moment when he walked into an ice cream parlour where a bunch of builders were having a rest, listening to some cool soul music blasting out from the juke box. Dave had never heard it before. One track in particular, by singer Ruth

Brown called 'Mamma He Treats Your Daughter Mean', caught his attention. Dave was desperate to catch the title of the record, as he fondly recalled:" I was trying to read the label as it went round and round and one bloke noticed that I was interested in it and pointed it out on the jukebox list. It was earthy, so real and the words so adult. This young man I wish I could go back and thank him now because it changed my life. He gave me five sixpences and said that if you like that then you'll also like this. Its called rhythm and blues, black American music."

And so Dave Godin's passion for soul music began in earnest. At Dartford Grammar school he met a young Mick Jagger and later on introduced him to black music. He also played a part in the early development of The Rolling Stones but he left because of how Jagger was exploiting black music. Upon leaving school he travelled around the States listening and educating himself to as much music as possible, during which time he also became a lifelong vegetarian. On his UK return he adamantly refused to agree to National Service and was given the sentence of working as a hospital porter, but that failed to derail him from his new true mission in life. 1963 was the year when Dave created The Tamla Motown Appreciation Society, with some help from Margaret Phelps, who was the president of the Hitsville International Fan Club. Upon joining, every member received a pin badge to wear, along with a membership card, and these are now highly prized, collectable items if you can find them - that is due entirely to the fact that there were only some three hundred members.

The young Dave managed to somehow weave his way into the Motown hierarchy so far that he was given the privilege of meeting people like Smokey Robinson's wife Claudette, along with two of the Marvelettes, Catherine Anderson and Gladys Horton. Despite all his tireless efforts, he was surprised to discover that the UK Tamla labels expressed scant interest in his ideas. Then out of the blue he received a telegram from Berry Gordy inviting him to an all-expenses-paid visit to Detroit to discuss plans for Tamla Motown expansion into the UK market. It is said that Gordy was very enthusiastic about Dave's plans and rewarded him with a job as a paid consultant to the rapidly expanding Tamla empire.

His genuine deep love of the music fuelled an even deeper passion for championing the cause, so he set up his own UK Tamla Motown label, which proved to be very successful. Now he was working for Tamla, success lay at Dave's feet and one would have thought that he would have been pleased with all the publicity building up at the time in readiness for the long awaited Tamla Motown Revue to hit the UK. Nobody was behind the idea as much as Dave; but instinct told him to take a step back and warn Gordy that the time wasn't right for a Motown tour. Gordy failed to listen to him and went ahead with the Revue, which turned out to be a complete financial disaster. Only the London show sold out and the tour was a massive worldwide source of embarrassment for Gordy.

Undeterred by the setback, Dave continued on his merry way, opening a record shop in Deptford in 1967 before moving to bigger premises in Monmouth Street, Covent Garden, called Soul City Records, from where he preached his soul gospel to his increasing flock of devotees. He later went on to create his own record label of the same name with help from two close friends, Rob Blackmore and Dave Nathan, who were both massively into soul music. They painted the shop in a distinctive shade of magenta and blue which were also the colours for the record label, with each single sold carrying the words "soul as deep as you like and then some." It was in Soul City Records where Dave Godin first coined the phrase 'northern soul', a name that replaced the rhythm and blues label - and how it came about is as entertaining as it gets. He had realised that more and more football fans from up north were visiting his shop and buying up these old soul singles as fast as they could get their hands on them. To save the staff any confusion, he told them to call the records 'northern soul' and the legend was born in a most terribly British way.

Soul City Records possessed all the knowledge, respectability and connections to have gone all the way but sadly this was not to be. Their single-minded love and passion for the records far outweighed their financial stability, and so the shop closed in 1976 after releasing only twenty singles, from artists such as Billy Butler, Major Lance, Billy Preston, Chris Jackson Erma Franklin, Don Gardner and Gene Chandler, who all went on to enjoy successful careers in their own right. Once again acting against Dave Godin's well intended advice, Gordy sent some of his biggest artists to return to the UK under the Tamla Motown Revue again, arriving on the 16th March 1965 with their first show taking place in the Finsbury Park Astoria before embarking on a gruelling nationwide tour, taking in twenty theatres twice a night, along with our own delectable Queen of Soul Miss Dusty Springfield.

With the help of Guy Stevens spinning the sounds in the Scene club, the pirate radio deejay Mike Raven and the *Ready Steady Go* producer, Dave managed to make the music he loved an integral part of UK culture, even stronger today than it ever was. There is a great photograph on the cover of *Dave Godin A Northern Soul* showing him sitting on a bench in Freedom Land adventure park in New York City, dressed in all white, talking to his hero Marvin Gaye, clear proof of how well he was accepted into the Tamla Motown hierarchy. The lifelong pioneer crusader of black American soul music died peacefully in Rotherham on October 15th 2004 age sixty-eight years old. Mister Dave Godin, soul as deep as you like and then some; and so we come to the first of the five clubs that continued on from where the original London rhythm and blues scene began.

THE CATACOMBS – AFFECTIONATELY KNOWN AS THE CATS – TEMPLE STREET – WOLVERHAMPTON – 1968 - 1974
THE DEEJAYS: IAN PEP PEREIRA, CARL FARMER DENE, ALAN SMITH, ROBERT CROCKER, ALLAN PRICE, FRANKIE BAGGOT, FROGGY TAYLOR, BLUE MAX

In terms of playing the latest northern soul singles, the Catacombs was second to none, punching well above its weight; so much so that somebody once called it the greatest little soul club in the land, lying somewhere between the the black rhythm and blues played at the Twisted Wheel and the fast tempo, sweat soaked energy of the Golden Torch. Had it not been for the club's small size and the fact that it didn't have that all-important all-night licence, the Cats would have definitely gone on to better and far bigger things within the northern soul scene. For only seven years the Cats lived a short but lasting life in a cramped, dark, run down former smelting works, where the only means of escape, should a fire break out, was down an old wooden staircase that had definitely seen better days. The only refreshment on offer, unless you brought your own booze into the club, was cold orange juice to quench your thirst.

The club's final closing night, which took place on the 13th July 1974, must have been one hell of an emotional night in the club's short history; those who were there must surely remember it forever. By all accounts they were crammed into a room with a vaulted ceiling large enough to hold five hundred people, when according to legend over a thousand turned up to say their goodbyes to the Cats. The place was like a furnace, so hot that people say some of the paint on the walls melted. People overcome with emotions were openly crying, others scratching their names on the garish coloured plaster walls. Apparently one epitaph read "It's the death of the Cats." Come the morning, it was the dreaded time for hugs, handshakes and kisses from the regulars, their pink membership cards strewn all over the dancefloor as the final record played: 'Where Have All The Flowers Gone' by Walter Jackson.

Of course a club can only acquire a great reputation if the right deejay and the right records come along and this was most certainly true of the founder member of the club, Mister Carl Farmer Dene, who was all that and so much more. Carl was one of the original staunch mods with attitude, who would never go to a club - even if the place was boiling hot - without wearing a shirt, tie and a sharp mohair suit. He was a deejay who had this unique ability to track down the rarest northern soul singles which the other deejays couldn't find for love or money. His passion and style for playing the latest rarest sounds kept the Cats dancefloor chugging along and begging for more, with many of his records finding themselves being played later in the Torch, the Wheel and Wigan, the demand for his latest discoveries going sky high as deejays jostled for the next new few sounds to pop out of his record box.

TWENTY CLASSIC TRACKS PLAYED IN THE CATACOMBS

SAXY RUSSELL - PSYCHEDELIC SOUL
THE AD LIBS - NOTHING WORSE THAN -BEING ALONE
JERRY WILLIAMS - IF YOU ASK ME
PP ARNOLD - EVERYTHING'S GONNA BE ALRIGHT
LEON HAYWOOD - RECONSIDER
TOO LATE - LARRY WILLIAMS - JOHNNY GUITAR WATSON
JJ BARNES - SAY IT
MITCH RYDER - YOU GET YOUR KICKS
EARL GUEST - FOXY
JJ BARNES - PLEASE LET ME IN

PEACHES - MUSIC TO MY EARS
VICTOR NIGHT - CHINATOWN
COD'S - MICHAEL
BOBBY WOMACK - WHAT IT IS
GENE CHANDLER - NOTHING CAN STOP ME
SHOWMEN - WRONG GIRL
BOB WILSON - SUZY'S SERENADE
FIDELS - TRY A LTTLE HARDER
SANDY WYNN - TOUCH OF VENUS

THE GOLDEN TORCH – HOSE STREET, TUNSTALL, STOKE ON TRENT – 1964 – 1973
THE DEEJAYS: KEITH MINSHULL, COLIN CURTIS, ALAN DAY, MARTYN ELLIS

There was one very special all-nighter which I would have given anything to be in the audience of on the night of Saturday the 9th December 1972, when Major Lance visited the Torch to record his live album of the same name. The Major was one of the artists the northern soul scene really loved and the four years he spent in jail in America for various cocaine related offences only increased his allure as a bad boy made good. The tracks on the album contained some of his big hits - 'Hey Hey', 'I Wanna Make Up', My Girl', 'Um Um Um Um Um Um', 'The Beat', 'Ain't No Soul', 'Investigate' and 'Monkey Time', the album being described as "perhaps the greatest northern soul album, a one off gig when everything came together in perfect harmony." As was the case when Edwin Starr came, saw and conquered the Casino, so the Major came, saw and conquered the Torch. All the tickets were sold out weeks before the big night and the cover of the album depicts the audience all squashed together, with most of them speeding their heads off, singing and clapping to the music. Admittedly not the most perfectly recorded live album, it was still a great musical moment in northern soul history and you can really feel the mood, the heat and the sweat. A cracking night was had by all, as I did alone in my bedroom singing and dancing to the Major's songs.

Wealthy businessman and music lover Mister Chris Burton was after buying a building to use as a live music venue when he came across the ideal building, which later became the Golden Torch. He paid around twenty-eight thousand pounds for the building, which had served the people of Tunstall well over the passing years being a church, a roller rink and the Little Regent Cinema. From a few photographs I've studied, the interior was a mini Casino with a dancefloor, balcony and pillars, with the decor being some kind of kitsch Roman style theme that kind of worked well. In the club's early days some big names played there: The Kinks, T Rex, Black Sabbath and Billy J Kramer. Thankfully that stage of the club's development all changed when Colin Curtis convinced Chris to put on some northern soul all-nighters. Chris agreed to give it a go and the rest is history, as the Torch held its first all-nighter on the 11th March 1973. In a room that could hold around five hundred people, apparently one night some thirteen hundred people turned up to check out what was going on at the Torch. According to a few people I've talked to, the live music nights went through the roof and some of the artists who played there included Oscar Toney Junior, The Drifters, The Stylistics, The Chi Lites, Inez and Charlie Foxx and Edwin Starr.

As time went on and more and more people were turning up to dance the night away, the once quiet neighbourhood was becoming more than a little disgruntled hearing the music, car doors slamming, engines revving, and people shouting. The local press featured an article exposing the flagrant amphetamine scene, prompting the police to take a keen interest in the place, hoping to bust a few people. On the 16th March 1973, the club applied to have its licence

92

renewed but the powers that be, sensing this was the perfect opportunity to close the place down once and for all, rejected the appeal; and that was the end of the Golden Torch. Some time later, rather like Wigan Casino, the Golden Torch was burnt to the ground by a mystery fire. It's gone forever but never forgotten.

TWENTY CLASSIC TRACKS PLAYED AT THE GOLDEN TORCH

ROSE BATISTE - HIT AND RUN
GENE CHANDLER - MISTER BIG SHOT
EDDIE PARKER - LOVE YOU BABY
DEAN PARRISH - I'M STANDING
SUPERLATIVES - I STILL LOVE YOU
FATHERS ANGELS - BOK TO BACH
LENNY GUESS - JUST ASK ME
JUST BROTHERS - SLICED TOMATOES
TEMPOS - COUNTDOWN HERE I COME
LEVI JACKSON - THIS BEAUTIFUL DAY
JIMMY THOMAS - BEAUTIFUL NIGHT
EARL WRIGHT - THUMB A RIDE
EXCITERS - BLOWING UP MY MIND
SOUL TWINS - QUICK CHANGE ARTIST
DARRELL BANKS - ANGEL BABY
BOBBY WELLS - LET'S COP A GROOVE
ROY HAMILTON - CRACKING UP OVER YOU
A QUITTER NEVER WINS - LARRY WILLIAMS - JOHNNY GUITAR WATSON

THE TWISTED WHEEL - CORONATION STREET BLACKPOOL - BRAZENNOSE AND WHITWORTH STREET, MANCHESTER 1963 - 1971

THE DEEJAYS: ROGER EAGLE, BRIAN PHILLIPS, COLIN CURTIS, KEITH MINSHULL, LES COKELL, BOB DEE, BARRY TURNER, BRIAN RAE, PAUL DAVIS

During a visit to the Twisted Wheel, the respected northern soul guru Dave Godin wrote the following words: "These are my kind of people, faint sounds of soul goes on because each and every one of us keeps the faith." One other simple quote sums up the Wheel: "No booze, plenty of blues." The actual building boasted an industrial heritage so Jack and Ivor Abadi, who owned the place, retained most of the original interior. Downstairs was a stage and a deejay area built like a cage of bicycle wheels and parts. The room had a number of alcoves and the walls were painted black, red and white, and the dancefloor was concrete, which must have proved painful for dancers pulling off their moves, not to mention wearing out their shoes. Upstairs was the cloakroom and the drinks bar serving up sandwiches and soft drinks.

The two main deejays in the early days of the Wheel were Roger Eagle and Brian Phillips, Eagle taking care of the blues nights while Brian deejayed the later all-nighters. What the two of them didn't know about RnB and soul music wasn't worth knowing about. Roger was a tall bloke, quite strange-looking, with wild eyes, who was really into his 50s and 60s rhythm and blues music the same way Guy Stevens was. The two became great friends, often meeting up to swap ideas and records. Roger loved the music so much he would have played the Twisted Wheel for free every night but that wasn't the point. The Abadi brothers only paid him three pounds a night and when he asked for five pounds, they refused to give him a rise, so he left to set up the Blue Note club and later on the Stazz Club in Fountain Street.

Brian's speciality was quality rare northern soul music and he boasted a massive collection of rare imported singles, introducing the Wheel crowd to sounds that were even rare in the States. He would often buy up five hundred at a time, hoping to find a few gems hidden away; which he always did. Indeed, his knowledge of soul music saved the Wheel when it was going through a dodgy patch, with the crowd feeling like the Wheel had seen better nights.

It is truly incredible the number of massive American soul artists who came to appear in a small, sweaty Lancashire club. It would be easier to name those who didn't play there but here are just a few of the soul music royalty that did play the Wheel: JJ Jackson, Mary Wells, Junior Walker, Robert Parker, Oscar Toney Junior, the Shirelles, Fontella Bass, James and Bobby Purify, Arthur Conley, Marv Johnson, Major Lance, Jimmy Ruffin, the Showstoppers, Johnny Johnson and the Bandwagon, Jimmy James, Edwin Starr, the Spellbinders and Geno Washington who appeared there on a number of occasions and who once said that of all the audiences he's performed for, the Twisted Wheel crowd were the most knowledgeable. My mate once booked Geno and the band to appear in Blackpool but the gig was badly advertised. Twenty or so people turned up to watch him, me being one of them, but Geno turned negativity around like only he could. So what if there were only twenty people? He went on to play a storming set of soul music lasting over two hours, just as if he was playing to a packed house. Back in Manchester, some old official bylaw stating that businesses weren't allowed to perform for more than two hours into the following day sealed the fate of the Twisted Wheel and it closed down in 1971; gone but never forgotten.

TWENTY CLASSIC NORTHERN TRACKS PLAYED AT THE TWISTED WHEEL

JIMMY SMITH - A WALK ON THE WILD SIDE
LAZY LESTER - I'M A LOVER NOT A FIGHTER
BERTHA TILLMAN - OH MY ANGEL
LITTLE WILLIE JOHN CHARLY - NEED YOUR LOVE SO BAD
ELMORE JAMES - IT HURTS ME TOO
SUNNY BOY WILLIAMSON - HELP ME
SUGAR PIE DESANTO - SOULFUL DRESS
JOHN LEE HOOKER - BOOGY WOOGY
RAY CHARLES - HIT THE ROAD JACK
ALVIN ROBINSON - DOWN HOME GIRL
DINAH WASHINGTON - TROUBLE IN MIND
MAJOR LANCE - UM UM UM UM UM UM
BOOKER T AND THE MG'S - GREEN ONIONS
JAMES BROWN - NIGHT TRAIN
JACKIE LEE - THE DUCK
JIMMY RADCLIFFE - LONG AFTER TONIGHT IS ALL OVER
BETTY EVERETT - GETTING MIGHTY CROWDED

WIGAN CASINO - STATION ROAD WIGAN - SEPTEMBER 1973 - DECEMBER 1981
THE DEEJAYS: RUSS WINSTANLEY, RICHARD SEARLING, KEV ROBERTS, MARTIN ELLIS, SOUL SAM, GINGER TAYLOR, BRIAN RAE, DAVE EVISON, KEITH MINSHULL, ALAN DAY, LES COKELL, IAN RIGBY, ALAN CAIN, IAN FISHWICK

From early 1974 up until late 1979 I was a paid up member of the infamously famous Wigan Casino soul club. Back then, if anyone had have told me that I would drop out of normal society and spend all my weekends in an old run-

96

down ballroom, dancing the night away, off my head on speed, to northern soul music, I would not have believed them. I was a cool teenager living in Blackpool, the Las Vegas of the north. Pubs, clubs, booze, birds and drugs, everything a fun-loving teenager could wish for, so why the hell did I give all that up and spend my weekends in that old ballroom when I had everything on my doorstep? It's a question I occasionally ask myself more than fifty years later. Strange, isn't it, that a small unobtrusive notice pinned to the wall of Scoeys soul club in Blackpool advertising places on the next coach to Wigan Casino - membership cards a must - can change your life, for better or for worse. It was a glorious early summer's evening back in 1974 when I boarded the coach to Wigan with my mates, carrying my all-nighter bag with essentials: spare tee shirt and trousers, ample cans of Tennents lager, a wrist sweatband, a can of Brut 33 and some black bombers to keep me bright eyed and bushy tailed when needed. Everyone was buzzing and a couple of lads were up and dancing in the aisle. It was a short journey over to Wigan, back then a dump of a town, as were many inland Lancashire towns, steeped in the crumbling faded heritage of the Industrial Revolution in which Wigan had played a massive part.

Slowly turning into Station Road, we pulled up outside the Casino, where a sizeable crowd had already gathered, some of them giving us angry looks as if to say "here we go, more daytrippers." Funnily enough, the same kind of angry looks we ourselves gave newcomers once we were established on the scene. Formerly the Empress ballroom back in the day, it looked singularly unimpressive, dilapidated and badly in need of some restoration. It was once the social hub of the town's population, where people met at the weekends, dancing, some falling in love and eventually marrying. Built in that opulent grandiose style the Victorian architects and craftsmen perfected, the Empress officially opened on the night of July 1st 1916. To celebrate the auspicious occasion, a grand, no-expenses-spared banquet was organised, attended by the social elite and town officials, and according to newspaper reports of the day, a memorable time was had by all. Meanwhile, over in France, there were no such celebrations as over fifty thousand Allied soldiers lay dead and dying in the clinging mud on the first day of the battle of the Somme. Judging from how badly the exterior had deteriorated over the decades, I seriously wondered what state the interior was in, as the old time honoured saying 'never judge a book by its cover' flashed through my head.

We left the coach and took our place in the queue, squashed up tight against the wall for a good half an hour or so, a tangible impatience in the air, with our holdalls on our heads to prevent the handles of our bags getting ripped off before finally the doors were opened and we started moving forward. The bouncers urged everyone to relax as they pulled us inside, pointing to a flight of stairs where we paid our fiver membership fee. Up some more stairs and through the flexible perspex double doors into the Casino, where I stood, completely mystified at the sight that greeted me and my mates. The sheer unbridled intensity of a Casino all-nighter in full gear, the incredible heat and sweat mixed in the smell of deodorants in the air as the sound of the Salvadors' 'Stick By Me Baby' blasted out from the front of the elevated stage area.

The dancefloor was absolutely rammed to capacity, everyone going through their fast, athletic moves without bumping into each other as I stood there speechless, taking in the action. Suspended above the dancefloor was a long neon tube strip-light that cast a weird ghostly glow over all of us. Anyone wearing white really stood out and it even affected the whites of our eyes. The interior of the building was of a bygone faded elegance, leaving me wondering what it must have been like in its heyday, couples in their best clothes dancing to full orchestras or perhaps enjoying a sneaky kiss and cuddle in the corner of the balcony while watching the action below, as we often did. A different generation, but little changes; only time. Because of decades of constant use, the carpet was sticky and well worn and the toilets a complete disaster, water always on the floor, water leaking from pipes reminiscent of a scene from *Titanic* but nobody seemed to give a toss. The toilets were only a pit stop, only a place to relieve yourself, towel down and change into some fresh kit before heading out to the dancefloor again. Just part and parcel of another Casino all-nighter.

That night almost fifty years ago changed my life forever. I can still easily remember it like it was yesterday, the music, the heat, the sweat and the dancing like some irresistible hedonistic cocktail of amphetamine-fuelled, predominantly working class culture at play. After the initial shock had worn off somewhat, we decided to head over to a quiet corner that became the Blackpool corner, our weekend home for every all-nighter and a perfect place to wind down and catch your breath after a energetic dancefloor session, just tucked far enough away from the madding crowd. For those of you who never experienced Wigan Casino, at times it could be a dark, dangerous place, with plenty of working class lads and hard with it, some having been detained at Her Majesty's Pleasure, where they learned a few invaluable habits to make life easier when they were released. We had many reports of lads getting rolled - mugged - for their drugs and cash by lads who wouldn't think twice of giving their victims a good kicking if they didn't play ball. One horrible night it was the turn of me and my best mate to get rolled. We were taking a quick leak down a narrow, dark alley when a mob of black guys appeared, blocking off the escape routes as one of them pulled a knife on us and told us the score. We could feel the knife points through our clothes, pressing against our flesh, as they emptied us of cash and drugs before disappearing into the night, leaving us relieved, as things could have turned out a lot worse for us if we'd have kicked off. The town centre was a dangerous place to hang out in and we soon learned to keep out of certain pubs where the locals didn't take kindly to strangers turning up in their pub drinking their beer, especially those wankers who were into northern soul. Quite a few lads had been jumped on by local yobs and ended up in the hospital getting treated. As Blackpool lads we learned to stick together and pick the right pubs to enjoy a couple of pints, or we cracked open a few cans in the open market waiting for the Casino to open.

The dancing in Wigan was out of this world, an energy-packed, unrehearsed choreography that would have given Bruce Lee a hard time keeping up with, leaving me strongly doubting that I would ever be able to dance like that. During those early all-nighters I could only watch from a safe distance, studying the moves to take home with me to practice in my bedroom. I quickly learned that there was a pecking order in operation on the dancefloor. The back of the floor was the domain of those like me, only setting out learning how to dance well enough to make it to the middle level. There were some great dancers in the middle section pulling off some cool moves but not quite good enough to progress to the ultimate level where Wigan's elite danced in front of the stage area below the deejays, who were banging out the sounds to keep them busy. The elite were the crème de la crème, lads and girls going at it like there was no tomorrow, some of the girls matching the lads' moves perfectly.

I spent countless hours in my bedroom learning to shuffle, spin, back drop and front drop until I told myself that I was now ready for my first appearance on the Casino dancefloor. Of course, reality supersedes fantasy, as I found out to my abject horror the first time out on the floor speeding and chewing away. The record playing is still one of my all time favourite northern soul classics, The Contours with 'Just A Little Misunderstanding', a nice mid tempo number for a beginner about to lose his dancefloor virginity, almost as if the deejay was giving me the perfect sound to show off my new skills.

I gingerly stepped onto the floor, and in the beginning all went surprisingly well as I eased myself into a cool, relaxed side to side back front shuffle in tune with the music. Seconds later I pulled off two fairly good spins, ending with a loud clap, and back into the beat as my confidence soared, prompting me to attempt something more daring. Going down into a backdrop, I came up, clapped, and went for a high kick, which turned out to be an absolute disaster. I was wearing my loafers at the time and they were a bit on the loose side… so I found myself watching my right shoe fly off my foot straight into the back of the girl dancing a few feet away from where I was. Talk about one of the most embarrassing moments of my life. She handed me my shoe back with eyebrows raised, leaving me to limp back to the comfort of the Blackpool corner with my head hanging in shame. A year or so later I was back out on the floor doing my own thing to 'You Get Your Kicks' by Mitch Ryder when I got a tap on the shoulder from the girl. "Glad to see you've improved since the last time we met, mate. Nice one."

For me personally, looking back to all those crazy, sweat soaked, amphetamine fuelled nights, the best years in Wigan for me were between 1974 to 1977 when nearly every record the deejays played became a dancefloor classic. The buzz phase going around at the time was 'northern soul' and interest in the scene and Wigan Casino in particular soared to an unprecedented level. Just as we had done a couple of years earlier, bus loads of fresh faces turned up to see for themselves what was happening in Wigan. It even featured on *Top Of The Pops*, much to my disgust. A bunch of Wigan dancers doing their thing to a truly diabolical instrumental called 'Footsee' that had nothing in common with classic northern soul tracks. Similarly there was a record by somebody called Nosmo King and The Javells, an abortion

101

of a track called 'Goodbye Nothin To Say', a title that echoed my feelings perfectly.

Running a normal nightclub can be fraught with unexpected problems so if you can, try to imagine running Wigan Casino where ninety percent of the members were off their heads on amphetamines. That responsibility fell squarely on the shoulders of owner and manager Mister Gerry Marshall and his assistant Mike Walker, who somehow managed to run an extremely tight ship the whole time Wigan remained open for business. Gerry and Mike were down-to-earth, great guys, always ready for a chat, or if you had something specific you wanted to ask them, operating from a cramped office in the back of the building. They respected us and in turn we respected them, so much so that a special place within the Casino was called Mister M's, dedicated to Gerry Marshall. It was a big enough room with a balcony above the dancefloor with an awesome reputation for playing the finest ultra-rare northern soul records for the purist audience insisting on the best of the best records care of the deejays Alan Cain and Ian Rigby. The temperatures on a packed night were nothing short of a tropical rainstorm and many of the Mister M's hardcore never ventured downstairs into the main hall, because the records they played, they claimed, failed to hit the spot. According to them, it was crap pop soul music, and that was Mister M's for you.

One night around summer 1976, Gerry interrupted the all-nighter to explain to us that he'd been approached by a guy from Granada Television who wanted permission to film a documentary in the Casino for the acclaimed series *This England*. He asked us to vote either yes or no to allowing them in to the Casino, which could so easily have done untold damage to the club with that being the last thing any of us needed. Nevertheless we voted for what turned out to be a really gritty, honest, down-to-earth documentary on what exactly made the Casino tick. The film crew took the time to interview Casino regulars who made clear the point that Wigan was their only escape route at the weekend after another grim working week. Highly commendable of *Granada Reports* for showing the real truth as to what was happening in the Casino instead of some journalistic clap trap sensationalising and focusing solely on the negative aspect of the Casino, which of course was the rampant amphetamine scene.

Talking of the massive amphetamine scene happening in the Casino, the reason why it was used so widely was because of the large audience and speed was dirt cheap. Back then, most chemists didn't have alarm systems, so for guys travelling to Wigan, there were plenty of chemists to choose from to rob without the hassle of getting busted by the cops. Demand always far outweighed supply so dealers had to really pull their fingers out to keep their punters happy. I remember a couple of nights in the Casino when there was a gear drought on, nothing around at all, and this lack of gear put a whole new different angle to the all-nighter, having to go straight instead of speeding our brains out. I seriously questioned myself as to the real reason I was into Wigan: the gear or the music? I'm not saying that the gear was better than the music, but that the two dovetailed together perfectly. One without the other felt like I was missing out on a good night.

A couple of good lads I knew who knocked out plenty of quality gear employed a novel approach when it came down to robbing chemists. Two or three drives around the block to make sure the coast was clear and then off they'd go with a piece of quality Axminster carpet. Once they were up on the roof and had located the glass skylight, they'd lay the carpet over the skylight and after three, both would jump, smashing through the skylight onto the floor below without injury. Once they'd located the dangerous drugs box, they'd wrench it off the wall with a crowbar and hey presto; next stop, Wigan Casino, looking forward to another brisk night's business.

Around late 1979 my time in Wigan Casino came to a somewhat abrupt end as a result of somebody showing me a photograph of myself standing next to a pillar in the Blackpool corner and I was somebody I barely recognised. Stripped to the waist, wearing my baggy corduroy trousers hanging from my waist, my rib cage clearly visible, hair swept back, sunken cheeks, my eyes big and bright like the headlights on an E Type Jaguar. It was the first time I'd ever taken a good look at myself in all the times I went to Wigan, and there I was looking like one of Bowie's Diamond Dogs as a myriad of memories flashed by... so there and then I made the decision that man cannot live on amphetamine alone, so I bailed, never to return, back to the old life I'd left well behind six years before.

I retain one fantastic forever memory of my time in the Casino and that was the night the great Motown soul showman himself appeared with his band: none other than Mister Edwin Starr. The word was out weeks before the gig, with all tickets sold, which meant that we were in for a hell of a night guaranteed. From the balcony to the dancefloor, the Casino was jam packed, and although no official figures were kept, from experience we gathered there were close to three thousand people, which would have been an all time record. The atmosphere was laced with expectancy as the show began with the appearance of his band dressed all in white, saxophone, keyboard, bass, drums and guitar laying down some ultra cool instrumental soul for a good fifteen minutes, priming us to receive the main man - and he didn't disappoint, walking out to tumultuous applause, visibly taken aback for a few seconds by our incredible response before throwing everything he had into a blistering performance that went on for almost two hours. All of us singing, dancing and clapping, matching him word for word, classic after classic, as if we were his backing band. I've seen some good artists in my time but that night Edwin Starr came, saw and completely conquered Wigan Casino, and we loved it - and what a great memory for me to sign out on.

TWENTY CLASSIC TRACKS PLAYED IN WIGAN CASINO

TOBI LEGEND - TIME WILL PASS YOU BY
JIMMY RADCLIFE - LONG AFTER TONIGHT IS ALL OVER
DEAN PARRISH - I'M ON MY WAY
THE SALVADORS - STICK BY ME BABY
CHRISTINE COOPER - HEARTACHES AWAY MY BOY
KIM WESTON - HELPLESS
THELMA HOUSTON - BABY MINE
FRANKIE VALLI - THE NIGHT
MARVIN GAYE - LOVE STARVED HEART
MITCH RYDER AND THE DETROIT WHEELS - YOU GET YOUR KICKS
TONY CLARKE - LANDSLIDE
THE CONTOURS - JUST A LITTLE MISUNDERSTANDING
THE MIRWOOD STRINGS - TEMPTATION WALK
FRANKIE BEVERLEY AND THE BUTLERS - IF THAT'S WHAT YOU WANTED
LOU PRIDE - I'M COMIN HOME IN THE MORNIN
JIMMY JAMES - HELP YOURSELF
LARRY WILLAMS - JOHNNY GUITAR WATSON TOO LATE
MAJOR LANCE - YOU DON'T WANT ME NO MORE
PP ARNOLD - EVERYTHING'S GONNA BE ALRIGHT
AL WILSON - THE SNAKE

THE HIGHLAND ROOM - THE MECCA
ENTERTAINMENT COMPLEX - CENTRAL DRIVE
BLACKPOOL 1965 - 1978
THE DEEJAYS: IAN LEVINE, LES COKELL, COLIN
CURTIS, TONY JEBB, STUART FREEMAN, BILLY
THE KID, PETE HAIGH

And so we have arrived at the final club call, the legendary
Highland Room, perched high up in the roof space of the
huge Mecca entertainment complex that was full to bursting
every weekend with out-of-town party people looking for a
good time, letting their hair down to dance the night away to
the popular commercial hits of the time while upstairs a
much more secretive, discerning crowd of people were
doing their own thing. The Highland Room was well named
due to the fact that it was one hell of an effort getting there.
There were two large, almost vertical escalators, one going
up and one going down, taking the people to where they
wanted to be; a dangerous ordeal at the end of the night,
especially with several pints of beer swilling away inside
you, clinging on to the handrail so as not to fall off. Then
you went down a long corridor that took you to the entrance,
double doors, above which the words 'The Highland Room'
welcomed you in.

The Highland Room was a welcome alternative to
the other northern soul clubs which were old, dark and dank.
The Mecca building was a newly built complex and the
Highland Room had the vibe of a clean modern discotheque.
From what I recall, the room was bright and airy with a
capacity to hold some five hundred people. There was a full
length bar to one side with the deejays tucked away at the
front of the room overlooking a great dancefloor, working
hard to keep the dancefloor full to brimming, with one
deejay in particular paying special attention to the scene he
played a big part in establishing. Mister Ian Levine hailed
from a wealthy family which owned the fabulous Lemon

Tree casino and discotheque, which brought a little touch of the famous Studio 54 to Blackpool. It was cool, elegant, plush, stylish and well-furnished, attracting a rich clientele, dancing to the latest disco sounds; it was a million miles away from the ordinary Blackpool pubs and clubs. Possibly because of his family's wealth, Ian often came across as cocky, arrogant and big headed, causing many people - me being one of them at the time - to dislike him immensely. It was born out of jealousy. Ian could have anything he wanted at the click of a finger and we all knew it. Luxury cars, designer clothes, finest restaurants, and holidays whenever he wanted, which amounted to everything we all wanted but didn't stand a cat in hell's chance of ever owning. For me, looking back to those times, the way he came across to people was born from his extensive knowledge of soul music so in many ways he could be forgiven for the way he was. He could have sat back and enjoyed the feeling of not wanting for anything but he didn't. He set out on a personal crusade to own every Tamla Motown single, and to help him achieve his dream, he travelled to America countless times, searching high and low not only for Motown but those far more elusive, rare rhythm and blues singles America didn't want, singles he knew full well would keep the dancefloor packed whenever he stepped up to record decks. It was his mission to keep the Highland Room exclusive and a cut above the rest of the clubs by finding the ultra rare, quality northern soul singles he was responsible for introducing to the scene. Many of the records Ian made successful he eventually passed on to the deejays in Wigan Casino, who had the reputation of giving their audience exactly what they wanted, which was fast, solid, storming 60s stompers they could not get enough of.

In view of this, Ian strived to be that little bit different in his approach to playing his records, always on the look out for something new, something groundbreaking. An example of this is that during one trip to America, he stumbled upon a record that he admits blew him away, which was a million miles away from the traditional northern soul played in Wigan. Later, back in Britain, he managed to buy a copy. He knew he was taking a chance because it was that different. The record was called 'It Really Does Hurt Me Girl' by a group called The Carstairs, It soon became a northern soul classic single that changed the whole Highland Room vibe, from the pace of the records he played to how well dressed the regulars were becoming, similar to an exclusive discotheque. Gone were the sports vests, the baggy trousers, ankle socks and flared skirts for a more sophisticated image that reflected the change in the new music, even down to the way people danced; although there was always one you could rely on to make sure he stood out from the crowd. A good friend of mine, Mister Rob Brightman, an avid Highland Room regular from the get go, was the kind of dancer with plenty of tricks up his sleeve, proving to be an awesome spectacle when he was in full flight. One party trick in particular he loved pulling off in front of the mesmerised crowd required perfect gymnastic balance and precision to stop him making a fool of himself in case things didn't go as planned. There he was, out in the middle of the dancefloor, enjoying a cool side back and forward shuffle before slipping into top gear, charging at the wall, legs and arms everywhere, executing a perfectly timed somersault, and then back into the soulful shuffle, leaving the crowd standing there in sheer disbelief and pulling in some nice looks from the ladies.

For a brief time, a state of war existed between the Highland Room and Wigan Casino, the former slagging off the Casino for playing white commercial pop music that was nowhere near proper northern soul. The Casino responded by claiming that their deejays were giving their audience what they wanted, adding that the Highland Room was a club full of posers, snobby elitists, a club for connoisseurs, an accusation that admittedly was partially true. Ian claimed that if a club has a future, then change becomes inevitable, essential, and if the Highland Room stood for anything, it was fresh, vibrant change.

Whenever people reminisce about those great nights in the Highland Room, one man's name repeatedly rises to the conversational fore: Mister Tony Jebb, one of the friendliest, most unassuming, extremely knowledgable deejays on the scene back then. We all loved and respected Tony, who always seemed to have an uncanny knack of playing what we wanted to hear at exactly the right time. He naturally loved to push the boundaries when it came down to the clothes he wore. One night in particular stands out in my memory, Tony walking in carrying his two boxes of records, his long hair all over the place, dressed in a see through white lace shirt and wide loons, looking like he didn't have a care in the whole world, posing the question we always wanted to ask but never did. "Well, is he or isn't he?" Had he been alive today Tony Jebb I'm sure would have been up there, an integral part of the other elder statesmen on the northern soul scene doing what he did best. Tony Jebb died from multiple sclerosis at far too young an age. RIP Tony, thanks for the memories.

Sadly, as the Wigan Casino attracted more and more people due to it having the all-night licence, the writing was on the wall for the Highland Room, which was forced to close down; but the memories, oh the memories are still there, leaving one unanswered question. If the Highland Room had been fortunate enough to have been granted the vital all-night licence, how would Wigan Casino have fared, facing such fresh, tough, loyal competition? A good few years ago, I was working in Galway when I heard the news from my best mate that Ian Levine was planning something special to be staged at the King George's Hall in Blackburn. I dearly would have loved to have been there but things just got in the way, a bridge too far and all that. The event was hosted by Ian himself to a packed audience, introducing the release of his deeply personal homage to the northern soul scene. Called *The Strange World Of Northern Soul*, it was a four CD collection featuring many in depth interviews with many of the people involved on the scene, including one hundred and forty-seven artists who all had northern soul hits in the UK, from artists, dancers and deejays. Ian personally financed it as well as spending God knows how many hours putting the thing together.

I watched the video a few years ago and it is an incredibly rare chance to be able to see the faces of the artists responsible for so many great northern soul classics. It was also a sad affair for me because clearly many of the artists had fallen on hard times, ripped off by record companies and agents and totally unaware of the value of their singles in Britain over the years. I've watched the videos and there is one humorous moment Ian recalled when he sneaked off from the Highland Room to check out what was going on in Wigan when he should have been playing his set. The manager of the Mecca noticed his absence and on his return he was called into his office for a serious heart to heart, making it clear to Ian that now was the time to make his decision: either stay in the Highland Room or try his luck in Wigan. Wisely Ian chose the Highland Room and the rest is history.

My mate told me that Ian had the final ace up his sleeve, bringing to the stage Bobby Paris, who was responsible for the classic record 'Nite Owl', which was the symbol of Wigan Casino. Older and frailer, apparently Bobby began singing but lost his way in the song, at which point the audience helped out, singing along to every word in what was a fantastic, passionate a cappella version of the song, with not a dry eye in the place.

Over the years I've listened to so many mixed comments about Ian Levine's brilliant documentary. Comments like "Who the hell does he think he is?" and "What's that video all about?" Well, in answer to the first question to all you good-for-nothing doubters slagging off everything from your sofa, Ian Levine played a massive part, a lifelong contribution to keeping the northern soul flame burning bright. He was the main man behind one of the greatest clubs on the scene and was responsible for introducing new singles which were almost lost forever, which he brought back from America and turned into dancefloor classics. In answer to the second ridiculous question, well, if you don't know, then you never will. His legacy to the northern soul scene cost him thousands of pounds, and as many hours, and only Ian Levine could have put together such a gargantuan, unique project. He managed to make it as personal and entertaining as possible and it is a truly outstanding insight into the strange world of northern soul. Well done, Mister Ian Levine. Love and respect from all of us. Being an upfront, openly gay guy, Ian changed direction in the eighties, becoming the main deejay for the gay club Heaven, where he commanded the record decks for the entire nineteen eighties as well as producing a string of hi energy music hits. He was responsible for working with some big name artists of that genre: Evelyn Thomas, Miquel Brown, Hazell Dean, Weather Girls, Pet Shop Boys, Bananarama, Erasure, Tiffany, Take That, Boyzone and Bronski Beat.

I was truly gutted to hear that Ian was suffering some bad health problems caused by a stroke that has left him paralysed down his right hand side. Despite this dreadful illness, he somehow found the energy and the time to turn up at a few northern soul nights, playing some of the music he has championed his entire life. Yes, being in the position he was in, he could so easily have sat back and enjoyed life's luxuries but he chose not to do so. He kept the scene fresh, vibrant and constantly changing via the records he brought back from America to play before British audiences. Well done Mister Levine, love and respect from all of us who were there back in the day.

TWENTY CLASSIC TRACKS PLAYED IN THE HIGHLAND ROOM

THE CHARADES - KEY TO MY HAPPINESS
LEROY TAYLOR - OH LINDA
THE AMBERS - I LOVE YOU BABY
THE CARSTAIRS - IT REALLY DOES HURT ME GIRL
SKIP JACKSON - I'M ONTO YOU GIRL
THE POETS - WRAPPED AROUND YOUR FINGER
VENECIA WILSON - THIS TIME I'M LOVING YOU
THE SUPERLATIVES - I STILL LOVE YOU
JIM GILSTRAP - RUN RUN RUN
THE ADMIRATIONS - YOU LEFT ME
ELOISE LAWS - LOVE FACTORY
JAMES FOUNTAIN - 7 DAY LOVER
ANNE SEXTON - YOU BEEN GONE TOO LONG
ILA VAN - YOU MADE ME THIS WAY
MAJOR LANCE - IT'S THE BEAT
LEE DORSEY - RIDE YOUR PONY
THE INCREDIBLES - THERE'S NOTHING TO SAY
SHIRLEY ELLIS - SOUL TIME
LARRY WILLIAMS - JOHNNY GUITAR WATSON A QUITTER NEVER WINS
THE VIBRATIONS - CAUSE YOU'RE MINE

EIGHT

Journey's end folks, and we have arrived at our last but certainly not least port of call in this story, featuring a fabulous, vivid, from-the-heart collection of anecdotes kindly contributed from an assortment of great people who have spent their lives on the northern soul scene. Most of the recollections come from an age before Facebook, Twitter, Tik Tok, Whassup and Instagram, which for me take away some of the mystery, magic and intrigue the northern soul scene has always had. In my opinion, one of the main reasons why the scene has remained so popular is because it has a real, genuine honesty about it and has never sold out to the suits, always managing to fly below the commercial radar. The songs tell stories about the good, bad and ugly moments we all share in life. Boy meets girl - girl meets boy - falling in love - marriage and a family before the split, leaving the pain, the tears and the heartache described perfectly in the song 'Too Late' by Larry Williams and Johnny Guitar Watson. Songs about leaving home for a better life, like the song 'I'm On My Way' and that brilliant anthem by Tobi Legend summing up just how short a stay we have on the planet, warning each of us to get out there, quit putting off what we want to do today because tomorrow we might not be able to do it, as time passes us all by without any of us realising it.

For the northern soul scene to continue to survive and flourish, it definitely needs young people to carry on from where we have all left off. Youngsters who really do want to be a part of this exciting, alternative, underground family. Youngsters who really want to learn to dance and gain knowledge about the records and artists we have to thank for the music they made that we have championed for over sixty years. There is a brilliant video on Youtube filmed

113

at one of the Blackpool soul weekenders in the stunning tower ballroom. The video is called 'Now That's How To Spin' and features the former world champion northern soul dancer Steve Cootes from Edinburgh dancing to a bluesy track 'I'm Shaking' by Little Willie John. Steve looks the part of a typical soul boy, sports vest, baggy trousers, leather shoes and a beanie hat, putting in a sublime performance, pulling off all the coolest moves with ease, poise and perfect balance, totally lost in the moment, singing his heart out to the words. Next to his right hand side is another dancer, an older gentleman dressed in white but still energetic with it. Okay, he's not pulling off spins, backdrops and kicks but his speed, balance, timing and footwork are up there with the best of them, easily keeping up with the music. To me, it's one of the best videos I've seen, two northern soul dancers decades apart yet both lost in the moment, a beautiful symbiosis of youth and age blending together as one.

One slightly worrying problem I have regarding the northern soul scene comes from me watching the rise in popularity of the Bristol Soul Club, all thanks due to one person who goes under the name of Soul Girl. From tentative steps I watched the young people getting some kind of feel for the music for the first time and from that moment, quite a few of them have matured into great dancers, with energy and passion, effortlessly pulling off all the right moves - backdrops - front drops - high kicks - spins - somersaults and shuffles - convincing me that the future of the northern soul scene is in safe and capable hands. What I don't like hearing about are these northern soul dancing classes Soul Girl is running. Dancing northern soul is all about spontaneity, individualism, timing and personal interpretation of a particular track playing at the time. Ask anybody where they learned to dance and you'd be laughed off the scene. Back in the day, we watched the dancefloor action from a safe distance, remembering as many moves as we could to take back home, where we'd spend countless solitary hours practising the moves as close as we could get them before even thinking of stepping out onto that hallowed Casino dancefloor. That first, tentative, heart-wrenching, do or die scary moment, hoping we weren't going to make a fool of ourselves; but if we did, nobody seemed to care less, a case of better luck next week. Ask Steve Cootes if he went to dancing lessons - yeah, right, I mean, what next? Northern soul line dancing? Uggghhhh.

GLENN WALKER FOSTER – LIFELONG MUSIC LOVER AND DEEJAY

'Can I get a witness…' This for me the iconic song that started my journey, which has lasted so far around fifty-two years. A journey full of ups and downs but certainly no regrets, my journey into soul music later to be renamed northern soul. I was adopted into a poor working class family and in 1968 I found myself being educated at Arnold boys public school in Blackpool on the north west coast of England. This was a testing time for me and for many boys from poor backgrounds and for me it was no different; however, music was. Like most boys in the school I was a big fan of bands like Cream, Pink Floyd, Led Zeppelin, The Kinks, The Small Faces and many others but for me one band stood out more than the others, this being The Rolling Stones. Mick Jagger is, was and always will be the penultimate entertainer. I listened to The Stones night and day as much as possible and the above song, 'Can I Get A Witness', was high on my list of personal favourites.

One day a pal of mine said "Hey Glenn, you're always singing that bloody witness song but have you heard it by Marvin Gaye." Not having listened to any Tamla Motown music, I inevitably replied in the negative, to which he offered to lend me the single, which I took home with me. After tea that evening out came the Dansette that I played the single on and Marvin Gaye's wonderful voice came rasping out of the speaker and BOOOOOOOOOM. Everything changed, and from that moment to this day, I'm still captivated by the sound of Tamla Motown. It just grabbed me hook, line and sinker, so much so that I used to sell my school dinner tickets to the fat boys and walk up to Bond Street coin shop, later to be renamed Melody House, where I met Eunice, who would sell me the latest Tamla Motown single every Friday.

Eunice was very kind to me and always gave me two singles for the price of one. She had another box in the shop with the word SOUL scribbled on it in felt pen and she suggested that I had a nosey, offering to let me take a few singles home with me and if I didn't like them, I could return them to her. Records like Dobie Gray 'Out On The Floor' and Gene Hatter 'Sign On The Dotted Line' and far too many more to mention, but I sensed that I was getting a good education in rare soul music and found my collection growing steadily for a fourteen-year-old former rock fan. Youth club discos were also playing Motown and soul, giving me the opportunity to hear some more of this catchy dance music that was capturing everyone's attention, who basically had had enough of the force fed pop music of the mid 1970s. I felt most fortunate as I loved all genres of music but Motown and soul added another string to my bow and I knew that Jagger was doing some cover versions of these great songs.

1973 and another piece of good luck fell my way when I was offered a part time job at the weekends and school holidays in a shop called Moochers in St Annes On Sea, where I lived at the time. The job was simple enough, all I had to do was stack records into piles under the shelving as well as keeping the place nice and tidy. All the records turned out to be American imported soul music on record labels like Cadet, Chess, Cameo Parkway, Neptune and many more. Saturday morning I was up stacking records when I noticed one in particular from Bunny Sigler with a B side called 'Always In The Wrong Place' that meant nothing to me but the A side was a song called 'Girl Don't Make Me Wait Too Long', a song I already knew about from my Bunny Sigler album *Let The Good Times Roll*.

I knew from a friend that this was a massive record and hugely popular on the soul scene and lo and behold there were fifty-two copies of the single in front of me. I could hardly contain myself and shot off to see the boss, a large Jewish man called Hector, politely asking him if I could take all the records instead of my wages. "You can have them all, Glenn, for a penny each." I knew that instant my life was going to change radically. I was already planning a trip to Wigan Casino in March 1974, a club that had recently opened that my pals who used to go to the Torch and Twisted Wheel were going to regularly. I decided to take all my copies of Bunny Sigler to Wigan and try to trade them off for other records equally popular at the time.

My favourite northern soul venue really has to be the Highland Room, Blackpool, above the Mecca, and for several reasons, mainly because it was only a stone's throw from where I lived. My great friend, the one and only Tony Jebb RIP, championed rare soul music at the venue along with Ian Levine and Colin Curtis and the quality of the records played in the Highland Room was outstanding, boasting one of the best quality sound systems in the country, so much so that it put some other clubs to shame. It was also a much more up to date, modern, cleaner club and this reflected in the clientele it attracted, especially the fashions worn. One girl we all knew spent all week making her own trendy outfits for Saturday night in the Highland Room. Every credit to the girl, who was never once seen wearing the same outfit twice in the years she was a regular in the Highland Room.

Over the decades I've been on the northern soul scene, I've had residencies playing records in

117

Wolverhampton, Worcester, Blackpool, Barrow In Furness, Lytham St Annes On Sea, Morecambe, Gateshead, Hartlepool, Newcastle, Newton Aycliffe, Middlesborough and many more. I'm also thrilled at having had chances to deejay at some of the scene's bigger venues like the International Soul Club Festival at Blackpool's Winter Gardens and Tower Ballroom. Over the years I've been lucky enough to form some solid friendships with people I consider to be extremely knowledgeable of this particular genre of music called northern soul: the late great Tony Jebb, Richard Searling and Colin Curtis. I was given the chance to watch and listen carefully to what these guys were playing and collecting, which turned out to be a great learning curve, not just for me but for any serious up and coming talent aspiring to becoming a serious soul deejay. Tony Jebb the entertainer, Richard Searling the consummate professional and Colin Curtis forever the ground breaker; and one more guy who deserves a mention is a great friend of mine, John Vincent, who was always a creative deejay.

Rare soul records, in my opinion, are all about falling in love, falling out of love, losing love and occasionally a social comment or story that somehow sticks with you for life. And so here I am in 2022, still promoting and deejaying soul music in Hartlepool and Middlesborough and various other places in the north east. Do I have any personal favourites? Yes, one or two, but then again I really do like all music of all genres so picking favourites can be somewhat daunting; but I can list a number of great rare soul records that I would most definitely class as my favourites.

OPEN THE DOOR TO YOUR HEART – DON BURDICK
NO SAD SONGS – JOE SIMON
BABY I DIG YOU – GENE ANDERSEN
THE BEAUTIFUL DAY – LEVI JACKSON AND SOLOMON KING

COME ON HOME – JACKIE EDWARDS
I GOT THE VIBES – JOSHIE JO ARNSTEAD
NOT TOO LONG AGO – UNIQUESS
THE ECONOMY – LEE MITCHELL
IF YOU AND I HAD NEVER MET – MAGIC NIGHT
TUCK A LITTLE LOVE AWAY – THE INTRIGUES
YOU'RE TAKING TOO LONG – BOSS MAN
LOOKY LOOKY – O JAYS
NOW YOU'VE GOT THE UPPER HAND – CANDI
STATTON
BREAKAWAY - TONI BASIL
ALL OF MY LIFE – DETROIT SOUL
EDDIE'S MY NAME - EDDIE HOLMAN
I NEED YOU – SHANE MARTIN
WE NEED TO BE LOVED – THE TEEN TURBANS
BABY I NEED YOU – MARSHA GEE

Of course in reality there are at least a thousand more records that will echo around my mind in this life and this beautiful soul music has found its way into my heart and the hearts of so many more people forever. GLENN WALKER FOSTER

IAN LEVINE - DEEJAY, PROMOTER, PRODUCER

I was born in Blackpool in 1953 and started collecting Motown records at the age of thirteen, and had decided that by the age of fourteen, I wanted to own every Motown record ever released. The guy who claims that he was the first rare record dealer was called Gary Wilde and he ran a cigarette kiosk on Victoria Street in the centre of Blackpool where all the mods would congregate as well as selling rare records. This was in the winter of 1967 to 68. Setting out to collect every record Motown released meant that some of the singles were very hard to find and people like Wilde took advantage of their rarity, charging four or five pounds a record. By the time I was fifteen I was going with my parents on holiday to America and finding very rare Detroit records in the shops and other places.

By the time the Torch closed in 1973 I had become a big name on the northern soul scene. I could look at the producer, arranger and singer and tell you straight away if it was going to be a ballad or a northern soul record but I wasn't very happy about all of it. By 1975 there were plenty of stomping 60s records still to discover but they weren't as good as the ones we were playing in the golden years of 1973 and 1974 when we turned up everything from Chicago, Detroit, Los Angeles and even Virginia. The overall standard was going down so it meant that when we found something we needed it. A perfect example of this is when we went to Miami in the summer of 1973 to 1974 and bought four thousand singles from old Salvation Army places for five cents each.

While I was there I heard a record on the radio by The Carstairs. They had a big hit on the Okeh label called 'He Who Picks The Rose' but this new record, called 'It Really Does Hurt Me Girl', absolutely blew my mind. It had this very throaty northern soul style vocal and feel to it but a slightly more shuffling beat, not so much as the Philly sound but a bit more dangerous for the scene. I tried to buy it but I couldn't find it in the shops and no one else seemed to have heard it. I went to the radio station and they said they'd been sent a demo copy from the record company Red Coach to be distributed by Chess records, who I phoned myself. They'd lost their distributor so the record had been shelved. I begged the radio station to sell it to me, telling them I was prepared to give them anything they wanted, but they refused because they liked it as well. I thought I was fucked.

Back in England, I found a dealer called John Anderson who'd moved from Scotland to Norfolk and I told him that I wanted this particular record. He'd just had a shipment in from America of one hundred thousand demos from various radio stations and gen hatter Andy Hanley, Bernie Golding and I went through them, and we found three copies of it. I would have heard the record in 1973 when it was first released but I didn't obtain it until 1974, and when we went back to Blackpool Mecca and played it, the whole northern scene changed.

After The Carstairs came this new wave of shuffling, hypnotic rhythms as opposed to 60s stompers stuff: Marvin Holmes 'You'd Better Keep Your Head', Bobby Franklin 'The Lady's Got Choice', Don Thomas 'Come On Train' and Jay Armstead 'I've Got The Blues'. Blackpool Mecca suddenly became the home of this new northern soul sound. It was wonderful for a while. The Wigan Casino crowd hated it and carried on playing their 60s stompers but when things like The Carstairs got played, the floor was much busier than when the stompers were playing. But what happened soon after was the bootleggers began to kill the exclusivity for us. Every rare record that we found, Eddie Forster's 'I Never Knew', The Glories' 'I Worship You Baby', The Sweet Things' 'I'm In A World Of Trouble' would all be bootlegged four or five weeks after starting to break in the clubs.

Our Golden Rule, which we applied in the Highland Room, was that as soon as a record was bootlegged, we would drop it like a hot brick. If three or four bootlegs were coming in every week, three or four original records would get dropped from the playlist and then three or four more had to be found to replace them. That meant that the quality of the sounds started to deteriorate. One of the biggest culprits was a guy called Simon Soussan, a massive record dealer, especially with what happened to 'Do I Love You' by Frank Wilson. According to Motown, they pressed up copies of the Frank Wilson single because he was producing for Brenda Holloway at the time. Gordy collared Frank back stage somewhere and said "Hey man, do you really wanna be an artist with all these hassles." Frank said "You're right, Berry, I'm not going to be an artist." So the story goes Gordy then destroyed all but three copies of Frank Wilson's single.

ADY CROASDELL - KENT RECORDS MAIN MAN, NORTHERN SOUL DEEJAY, PROMOTER, COLLECTOR

My first experience of northern soul was at Kelmarsh, Northants, only four miles from my home town. It started off as a poorly attended soul disco playing Stax Motown and Geno etc but at midnight it turned into the coolest club ever. A hundred skinheads descended on the place with copies of The Esquires, Tony Clarke, The Fascinations and many more records, opening up my eyes to a whole new world. Next up was Bletsoe, Bedfordshire. Okay, so Kelmarsh was only a disused railway station but this place was a genuine old barn, the decks powered by a generator brought in for the night, and the floor was rough concrete covered in dust after a couple of plays of 'I Don't Want To Discuss It'.

The Lantern in Market Harborough meant all-nighters finally in my home town, where I exerted my musical influence by asking the DJ to ditch 'Knock On Wood' and play 'The Right Track' by Billy Butler. Martin Ellis and the Manchester smoothies came down with copies of 'A Quitter Never Wins' – Real Humdinger and 'Hooked For Love' for which my mate paid four quid, which was totally incomprehensible for me.

The Torch in Hanley near Stoke, going up with the second known copy of 'Time's A Wastin' by The Fuller Brothers with Dave Burton which got us the VIP treatment. My biggest all-nighter to date but I still preferred the local smaller do's even though we didn't have a copy of 'Inky Winky Wang Dang Do'. Saints and Sinners in Birmingham, the ultimate underground in the middle of the city centre.

You had to walk through an all night café filled with people only slightly less dubious looking than ourselves, through a door and along several corridors into the bowels of the earth. The final door would open and you'd see a small, red-lit room with a minimal dancefloor and fifty to a hundred people of your own all-night crowd.

The Birds Nest, West Hampstead was only an evening do with Dave Burton, Dave Rivers and Mick Smith the DJ playing some of the best and biggest sounds of the time. The Catwalk – 'I Got Something Good' and' Just Like The Weather'. Very large green chairs, Carlsberg Special Brew and Mandies from the only five strong skinhead gang at London University at the time. Keen but messy. The Pier, Cleethorpes, arriving to hear the dancefloor bouncing up and down in a very unique style. It had to be 'The Champion' by Willie Mitchell and it was. Why was I so popular after my first stateside trip, flogging 'Love Factory' for three quid and Shane Martin for four? Yate Bristol in deep snow, surely nobody would have made it tonight. We were even certifiable for trying. The car-park looked dead but inside five hundred people were dancing like maniacs to DJ Clarkie playing a few sounds I'd passed on to him like Frankie And Johnny and Kiki Dee etc etc.

Wigan and the Big Un! I went on one of the first nights and enjoyed it but it was a bit too big and sparse. A year later it was too big and crammed. The crush on the door, the volume of people, the heat, the records, it all made it slightly surreal. We were the boys in the record room probably for the first time. I can't remember any vinyl dealers at The Torch. The DJs seemed to have a few ego problems and they sat on the stage with their wives and girlfriends and favoured friends like a gathering of minor royalty. It was a bit beneath them to visit the record room and they generally sent their minions to find the sounds they wanted. It was a great experience but I lost my respect for the place when Mick and I found the dreaded Tony

123

Blackburn LP down Portobello Road. Cut the Lenny Gamble acetate 'I'll Do Anything' and not only did Minsh play it but the divs danced to it. No thanks!

A boozer in Hammersmith, West Hampstead, Randy and my second venue where we consolidated the crowd and turned a generation of mods on and still had fun. Probably typified by the cover 'For Dancers Only'. The black guy was a taxi driver who'd come to pick up the bouncer who'd just let off a fire extinguisher in the toilet. We got closed down and the place became too ridiculous for the management to handle. Kenny Carlton, Caroline Nash and Johnny Nash. Stafford next and more musical learning. Where did all those new records come from? I thought they knew about northern soul but who changed the playlist? A whole new set of friends, many of whom last to this day. This is the hardcore of the scene who keep on going regardless. Tommy Navaro, Eddie Day and Peanut Quacking Duck.

The 100 Club, DJ fights, girlfriend and sister fights, rockstars in the cloakroom, people travelling down from Yorkshire and Lancashire to hear northern soul records being played exclusively in the smoke. All guest all-nighters letting the punters play the records for the first time. First female DJ since Guy Stevens club in the 1960s. Ridiculous amounts of anniversaries followed by anniversary singles. Things becoming boring, having to be responsible to keep it going. I couldn't be one of the lads anymore, learning to be a DJ. Latin, soul, big ballads and unissued master tapes the regulars. Real people – thanks!

BOB CUMMINGS - NORTHERN SOULER, TWISTED WHEEL

I first visited the Wheel on my sixteenth birthday, 17 October 1964. Admission to the Wheel was two and sixpence on a Monday night to see Alexis Korner and a bit more expensive for top line acts on Saturday nights including Sonny Boy Williamson and Steam Packet with Rod Stewart. Top acts who performed at the Wheel included Edwin Starr and Geno Washington and his Ram Jam band. There were many blues tours at the time, and soul firmly had its roots in the blues, and rhythm and blues, that all the British groups were doing copies of. Soul was beginning to emerge with the Isley Brothers, Stevie Wonder and the all-girl groups, The Shirelles, Shirley Ellis, and the Marvelettes, who appeared at the Odeon on Oxford Road.

I've mentioned briefly the old Twisted Wheel in Brazennose Street and the new Wheel in Whitworth Street but what about the Twisted Wheel in Blackpool? I joke not. The Manchester Wheel was run by brothers Jack and Ivor Abadi and their dad ran the Blackpool Wheel. Downstairs was just like a typical cafe and used to fill up with mums and dads after a cup of tea. Upstairs there was a jukebox, a dancefloor and a deejay area. The first track I heard going up the stairs was "Hey hey, I'll be sending out an SOS." Once some scooter boys followed the coach over to Blackpool and parked up outside the Wheel. The craze that week was schoolcaps and they all them on with their parkas. Cool or what? Also Levi 501s were becoming the thing to wear, preferably with a white Levi jean jacket, so all you Wigan northern boys know that your roots come from the mods.

I went to my friend's one day and left with a deep depression. He was playing *Sergeant Pepper*. Some became hippies when the Wheel lost its edge, others mourned the fact that their short haircuts were adopted by the crazy loony terrace skinheads. The rest of you up the East Lancs road to Wigan.

DAVE PHILLIPS - DEEJAY, TWISTED WHEEL

The Wheel was slowly moving from its roots in folk jazz and the blues and RnB, becoming the originator of northern soul, due to the two brothers who managed the club and the legendary deejay Roger Eagle, who introduced a whole new generation to Jimmy Smith, Sonny Boy Williamson, Little Walter, Elmore James, John Mayall, John Lee Hooker and more. The club was a coffee bar, no booze but lots of blues. After a Saturday night with Alexis Korner, Georgie Fame, John Mayall, and Eric Burden, who can forget the Sunday morning hikes in the Peak District after the all-nighter?

In 1963-1964 the influence of soul became dominant with the rise of Stax and Motown. The mod scene was here, fashions changing weekly, pop music influenced by blues' rare records. Everything connected with blues and soul was rare in those days. The radio did not play soul and hardly any record shops had heard of artists. "Green Onions. You want the grocer's shop mate." In any case, black musicians was seen as not quite the thing; but that sort of attitude simply encouraged us. Junior Walker, Edwin Starr, Oscar Toney Junior, Marv Johnson, Mary Wells, Ike and Tina Turner, John Mayall, Johnny Johnson and the Bandwagon, Geno Washington and the Ram Jam band were just a few of the artists who appeared in the Twisted Wheel.

BENNY ROBERTS - TWISTED WHEELER

I was sixteen at the time, living in Stockport with my mates, and we called ourselves the Stockport Wheelers, drinking there until they called time and then we'd head for the Twisted Wheel for the all-nighter. The age range was between fifteen and seventeen, although there were a few girls there who were as young as fourteen. It was a great way for us to let loose because there were no adults there, no

126

parents, so we could do what we wanted and go where all the mods were heading for. You also never told your parents where you were going because the Wheel was always in the papers about drug raids. The main thing about the Twisted Wheel was that you couldn't hear these uptempo records anywhere else. It certainly wasn't on the television or radio and that's what attracted people.

MIKE EASTWOOD - TWISTED WHEELER

I remember being there on the closing night. Word had gone round that the Wheel was famous for drugs and there had been many break-ins in chemists shops all over the place which became one of the reasons why it closed down. The Twisted Wheel was a mod club, which was the number one culture back then in the 60s. You went to the Wheel because it played some great music and the drugs just added something to the evening. Overall it was very much a working class culture. Its notoriety for being a place of drug-fuelled dancing ultimately led to the club's demise. This was due to the many police enquiries into the rampant amphetamine usage that the dancers needed to last all night and the burglaries in local chemists for these type of drugs which finally put an end to the Twisted Wheel all-nighters.

PETE ROBERTS - TWISTED WHEELER

I used to go to the Twisted Wheel when I was only a kid, just before I left school in 1968. The only problem with it was that it had a really bad name. When I first went to the Wheel, I really thought that I'd sold my soul to the devil. I couldn't believe that I was actually in the club and to be honest, it wasn't all that bad, but it still had a bad name and famous with it for amphetamines, and ultimately the police really wanted to close the place down. There was a lot of amphetamine use and dare I say one of the reasons people went there because when you were out all night dancing, you needed something like that.

MARK SARGEANT – JOURNALIST, DEEJAY, RECORD COLLECTOR, NORTHERN SOULER

Looking back at my formative years when I was a teenager is unnerving, some of the things that were normal. Discovering girls, clothes, beer, fags, football and music all within a few months of each other. Ok football wise I'd been indoctrinated into supporting my local team, Oxford United, from the off by my dad. As I became a teenager I'd go with the lads and get involved in both home and away excursions. Adopted or tolerated by the local skinheads, who all had at least three years on me. I learnt to ride scooters, Lambrettas, and would bunk off school on Wednesdays to work on a market stall. Not just any old market stall, this one offered Levi jeans, Sta Prest trousers, Ben Shermans, Brutus and Jaytex button down collar shirts as well as Harrington jackets and Crombie style coats. A handy way of earning a few quid as well getting a huge discount on all the clobber. Eventually my school had enough of my antics, which resulted in me being expelled a few months before I was fourteen.

As for the music, in the very early 70s it was Trojan reggae, Stax, Atlantic and Tamla Motown. There was a youth club in Oxford city centre called the Catacombs and it was in there I made my debut as a deejay. For me the soul side just shaded it, especially as it was soul music that all the girls seemed to prefer. Early 1972 I had my first encounter with what would become known as northern soul. A car full of us had been to an away match and on the way back, at the insistence of Coco a suedehead from Bicester who went to the Golden Torch, we stepped off in Wolverhampton at a place coincidentally called The Catacombs. I'd have been fourteen at the time, full of alcohol and pharmaceuticals, and I can't remember much about that particular experience apart from it was hot and dark and the music seemed to be absolutely brilliant. Mind you, I was trying out all my best chat up lines which for once failed me every time.

Saturday nights, football away days excepted, were often spent in Dunstable's California Ballroom, a bit of a trek from Oxford but even with a midnight finish most nights we spent in the 'Cali' were excellent. There was always a live act in the main room, invariably an American soul act. I saw Arthur Connelly, Ben E King, and The Sunshine Band, George and Gwen McRae, Edwin Starr, The Four Tops, The Temptations and many more. Downstairs was the Devils Den where resident DJ Brother Louie served up the hottest new import 45s. Working in what was for a short time Oxford's cutting edge menswear outfitters, the Stag Shop, where every day the music played in the shop on the eight track was soul. Baggies both pleated and high waisted as well as bowling shirts, leather bomber jackets and three quarter length coats were all available off the shelf. I'd occasionally browse through the assistant manager's copies of *Blues and Soul* and *Black Music* magazines, in which Tony Cummings' first northern soul special started off with Eddie Foster's spirit visiting the underground UK scene which had quite an appeal. Russell Acott's, a music shop that stocked a massive amount of soul music in the upstairs record emporium, both old and new imports, proved to be very helpful. In the *Black Music* magazine, a feature was a playlist from scenes past of which the northern soul scene sounded interesting, so naively I enquired if any of the records were still available. On British release from stock, among my acquisitions were Bobby Sheen's 'Doctor Love', The Poets' 'She Blew A Good Thing' and Bobby Hebb's 'Love Love Love'.

Fellow Oxford United supporter Graham Hilsdon dropped into the Stag Shop one day late September 1973 informing me that there was a coach trip to Wigan Casino arranged for early October and was I interested in going. You bet I was, so I started spreading the word around and all the seats were snapped up quickly. The membership card arrived shortly after, a blue one which I still have today and so it was, a few weeks after the Casino's first anniversary, I made my first trip to the all-nighter, which was a defining moment in my life; taking my first look off the balcony at the packed dancefloor below, I was hooked. Even though the windscreen on the coach shattered on the way back to Oxford, I wasn't put off. As clichéd as it sounds, my first visit to Wigan Casino was a life-shaping moment.

Excursions to the Casino were every four to six weeks and some of my early original purchases included Gwen and Ray's 'Build Your House On A Strong Foundation', Christine Cooper's 'Heartaches Away My Boy' and Williams and Watson's 'Too Late'. While my visits to Russell Acott's turned up lots of gems, a chap called Brian who worked there the weekends had been buying up Tamla Motown for years, which led to some nice UK items joining my collection, the cream of which was Kim Weston's 'I'm Still Loving You' on Tamla Motown TMG511 white demo disc for a large brandy.

I'd changed my job by then, working as a bar manager in Oxfords then at top nightclub Scamps, a classic uptown late night meat market that was part of the Star group, who had a whole complex of premises close to Blackpool's North Pier as well as a chain of clubs across the country. Work commitments, as in two-thirty to three in the morning finishes, six nights a week, didn't allow more than one monthly night off to allow me to travel north for a few hours in the Casino. Train hitching, the Portsmouth coach, minibus and car convoys meant that we all got to Wigan a variety of ways. John 'Kojak' Harvey with his Inter City

Soul Club, which was a kind of travelling roadshow, was quite active at the time so I blagged myself DJ spot at the Oxford All-Dayers which were staged on a Sunday more or less. He also started putting on all-nighters in Yate near Bristol, which was only around a fifty mile drive to get there. I attended most of the Yate all-nighters under Kojak and The Southern Soul Club banner and finally Mick Macavoy, who before Yate held several all-nighters at a hotel in Swanage. Yate night lights would go on in Scamps and from nowhere a horde of guys and girls in wide trousers and flared skirts and eyes as wide as their strides and chewing gum invaded the place. Collecting, washing and restocking the bar while I cashed up before shooting off to Yate, which was a ten mile drive away.

Also during the Yate era, I attended most of the Bisley Pavilion all-nighters while in Abingdon. The youth centre wanted to raise funds for an all-weather five-a-side football pitch so they oversaw the monthly all-nighters and the occasional all-dayer as well. Occasionally I would take a trip to The Lacy Lady, The Goldmine and The Rio in Didcot where I guested as a warm up deejay several times. Saturday lunch time sessions in Scamps back in Oxford, where we played one hundred percent imports and promo only British pre-releases were popular. That was my baby for the years it ran, with people coming in from a thirty to forty mile radius. Mind you, at the time Oxford boasted some excellent clothes shops as well as Russell Acott's record shop stocking all the latest US imports. I guested at the jazz funk all-dayers in Reading, remembering a moment when Chris Hill led a Conga through the main room and put 'Magic Fly' on the turntable prompting Cockney Mick to snap it in half.

During the Golden Era I only managed to make it to the Blackpool Mecca a few times with Cleethorpes Pier and St Ives being two more venues I visited even less. The Abingdon all-nighters proved popular even though the venue was strange to the point where many people christened it the Goldfish Bowl, but there were plenty of rare original singles available at a reasonable cost. For me, Wigan never disappointed. Bisley was always fun and Yate was excellent. The card schools and the backgammon as the sun filtered through the curtains to a backdrop of rare, top quality soul music and I'd go as far to say that Yate at its peak laid down the blueprint for the Stafford style sounds. After I had changed jobs from working at Scamps, a typical Yate excursion went something like this: meeting up in Abingdon, from where several cars would head off together to Newbury, descending on a pub called The Anchor or maybe The Ship where the local soul fraternity had stocked up the jukebox with a load of northern soul reissues. When Yate was going on, it became a magnet for most people travelling west to Yate pausing for a pit stop at the Leigh Delamere services, where we'd meet up with other people who were Yate bound.

In 1978 I acquired a Lambretta GP 125 and within twelve months there was a sizeable number of us travelling by scooter to the early 60s rhythm and blues soul nights in Hemel Hempstead. All-nighter wise, things started happening fast in Peterborough, Stafford, Chesterfield, the 100 Club, Leighton Buzzard, and later on The Bradford Queens Hall. I was getting regular deejay work by then at the Bradford all-nighters as well as a number of guest spots in other venues. Workwise I'd gone back to electrical engineering, with a steady five day week of only thirty-nine hours which freed me up to enjoy more leisure time, so I could get to as many soul nights as possible. I was also doing the national scooter rallies, competing in events as well as going to as many Oxford United games as possible. Wembley 1986 was the pinnacle of the Yellows' success in the first division and League Cup win.

Although I'd always swapped and sold singles, it was during the 1980s, like many other soulies, I started to prune many classic northern soul singles from my collection. Having a cosmopolitan taste in my music, many went in for swaps to fund the purchase of more rare singles. The Canal Tavern was a superb soul night with Dave Dearlove the man in charge, in addition to which was a real soul goldmine with the quality of music played there ultra high. I'd been asked to contribute to a brand new scooter magazine called *British Scooter Scene*, which eventually became *Scooter Scene* before merging with *Scootering Magazine*. Marriage broke, I was freelancing for the local paper as well as a number of other publications so I took voluntary redundancy from the factory to go where my heart longed to go. I visited venues such as The Hacienda and The Ministry Of Sound after going to a few of the early raves, which were similar to the northern soul scene, but when you've found your own brand of champagne, others may well be similar without actually pressing any of your buttons. Bizarrely I ended up promoting live music; that I managed to mix in with work commitments, so the soul end of things went on the back burner for a few years. One of the venues I worked for followed my suggestion to introduce a night called "Retro" with the format comprising of classic soul and funk, which proved to be unbelievably popular, giving me a smug satisfaction, listening to music from Carol Anderson, James Fountain, Glenda McCleod and many other soul classics I introduced to a brand new audience.

Once you've been bitten by the rare soul bug you stay infected and there is no cure. The Metropolitan Soul Club started to hold all-nighters at the Rocket Inn in North London, an excellent venue with some superb obscurities but a big shame regarding the northern soul scene's politics. I was a deejay at a couple of the warm up sessions across Holloway Road as well as a guest spot at one of the all-nighters followed by the opportunity to deejay the Togetherness soul weekends in Fleetwood a few miles down the coast from Blackpool. Since that time I've been buying and selling rare soul records and there is still a handful I'm searching for if the price or deal is right. In recent years I've guested at Bisley, the Talk of the South and the Aylesbury soul nights. Over the years I've managed to amass over ten thousand singles and twelve thousand twelve inch singles and LPs on vinyl not to mention CDs as well, the vast majority of which are rare soul records. Even now I can't resist ferreting through second hand vinyl whenever I encounter it. Still collecting, still enjoying and still, when I can, getting to various soul nights and all-nighters more years later than I prefer to admit to.

ROB BRIGHTMAN – LIFELONG NORTHERN SOULER

When Pete asked me to contribute some memories to include in this book, my head went into overdrive, virtually writing its own book. I'm a recovering alcoholic with thirty-one years sobriety behind me which doesn't help much but explains why because of my many "black out" sprees suffered over the years. That is, I drink, I perform and act naturally as best I can, except that I'm left with no or at best sketchy memories of some of the events over the course of my life.

What I do remember was at the age of twelve my dad sent me to St Paul's youth club on Preston Old Road, Blackpool, where I heard an older boy called Mark playing 'You're Ready Now' by Frankie Valli, when I experienced my first "tingle" that sent a shiver down my spine and covered me in goose bumps, something I'm told only really happens to some ten percent of people. Mark explained that it was soul music – the term northern soul wasn't used back then – as he slipped the single back into its white cardboard sleeve with the title of the record and artist neatly written in the top corner. As daft as this sounds, that minute moment changed my life forever.

Part of my illness over the years is that I obsess over many things, which I did with seven inch vinyl soul music singles. There were many rumours flying around Blackpool that an album was due out featuring some local lads on the front cover. Turns out that that album was the classic Skinhead *Moonstomp* which in turn became my first ever pre order album. Fast forward a few years and I was at an under eighteen disco on Chapel Street where I first met Roy Ashworth – Tache – who was one of the older lads featured on the cover of the *Moonstomp* album. Roy was a main face on the new northern soul scene and an absolute sublime dancer to say the least. To this day, the best I've ever seen, and as a kid watching him dance to 'One Wonderful Moment' by the Shakers or 'Tell Me It's Just A Rumour Baby' by the Isley Brothers, encouraging me to learn how to dance myself, was such a powerful life changing gift and one I'm still in awe of today.

As a result, I spent countless nights up in Blackpool's legendary Highland Room in the top of the Mecca building. How we were allowed in so young was amazing and during this time my eternal love for northern soul was born. Anybody who was a regular in the Highland Room who doesn't rate the late great Tony Jebb on their list of the top five deejays knows nothing about northern soul. Further afield, the famous Twisted Wheel on Whitworth Street in Manchester was as near as I was going to get to heaven and the club still holds a very special place in my heart.

Meanwhile, back in Blackpool during my early northern soul apprenticeship, my other favourite venue was the Peacock Room on Cherry Tree Road, a small venue boasting some great deejays playing great soul music and the chance to meet some of the local Okeh scooter crew, who were absolute legends back then and still going strong to this day - as is my love affair with northern soul, still feeling my heart beating faster when I listen to 'Queen of Fools' and other such fantastic tunes.

The modern northern scene has taught me that we need as many of the obnoxious people on the scene for us who were there back then to appreciate just how magical and special the real people were back in the day and for me personally, how the countless memories as a result of meeting those people and those times blessed my life so much. Meeting some gorgeous human beings as well as hearing and loving the music with an undying passion, which for me is infinitely better that any medicine I've taken over the years and long may it continue to be so.

One thing from back then that still remains an indelible memory, yet at the time became such a part of normal life: Saturday mornings up at the crack of dawn, rushing to Sinfonia Records on Cookson Street, spending time with the owner Sandie Mountain, a friendly, knowledgeable guy who knew just about everything there was to know about American soul music and then some. If he didn't know about it then it wasn't worth checking out. Every week a brand new stock of imported singles would arrive so it was imperative to be the first one through the door. I remember buying 'What' by Judy Street for the princely sum of forty-five pence on the red Strider label. I spent many hours in Sandie's vinyl empire thoroughly enjoying the banter and the camaraderie that went on in there, leaving me with so many great memories hanging around like-minded people.

As I've got older it's just nice to see pals who were there all those years ago, especially the scooter lads who are still driving and dancing. What I've noticed over the passing years, I've learned so much more just how much the drink and drugs affected me that all my nights spent on the scene were similar to a trailer for a big movie three hours long, full of fleeting memories, remembering places, faces and records. I don't need people to believe how many times and how many places I went to because I know I'm full of so many great happy memories of the times back then and the tunes I've heard a thousand times and more, still feeling the same passion and warmth.

The feeling I get deep down inside cannot be put into words. Tunes I know inside out and upside down, some of which are cheesy and definitely not text book northern soul but I still love them to this day not for their musical quality but for the feeling inside that comes over me each time I hear them. 'My Heart's Symphony', 'Pain In My Heart', 'I've Been Hurt', 'I Go To Pieces', 'Love Love Love' and 'Queen Of Fools'. Believe me when I say this but those tunes are so essential, if not more so, to my well being as any medication I've taken or step programme I've been on.

KEV ROBERTS – WIGAN CASINO DEEJAY, MANAGING DIRECTOR GOLDMINE RECORDS

I grew up in Mansfield and in my early teens I started going to youth clubs and discos. Hardcore working class towns like Mansfield were very mod, skinhead and Motown influenced and the first time I ever came across northern soul was in a place called the Folk House in 1968. There were a couple of real heroes there called Dave Presolloc and Paul Harrison and they played things like 'Our Love Is Getting Stronger' by Jason Knight and 'I Feel So Bad' by Jackie Edwards, which were two singles that were impossible to get hold of when I was still at school. In 1970 I got tipped off that there was a small stall selling records in Mansfield market run by Brian Selby and John Bratton, who went on to create the Selectadisc record label. Every Saturday afternoon their stall would be full of soul boys far and near who'd come to snap up all the latest releases.

In late 1972 I got my first job as a deejay at a club in Nottingham called The Brit with a small box of records which I'd been collecting since leaving school. I couldn't even cue up a record properly but I'd been buying about two imports a week since leaving school and had a nice little collection, so I started playing The Brit and the crowd remained. It was about that time when Alan Day, who used to deejay at Up The Junction, became a big name on the northern scene and just before leaving Selectadisc he took me to The Torch for the first time. December 1972 and my first real introduction to the scene. The place was packed that night and my head was spinning. I didn't know half the records they played even though I knew quite a few. Then suddenly The Younghearts' 'Sliced Tomatoes' and 'Please Let Me In' were played. I'd never heard them before and I thought it was wonderful. The next week I got the train, which was a hell of a journey. We were waiting at the door at eight o'clock and from then on I was hooked.

Then one week after the Blackpool Mecca – the Highland Room, the lads told me they were off to Wigan and asked me if I was with them or not. So off to Wigan Casino it was, with my box of records which I took to show off to people. It was September 1973 and as I walked through the doors I thought," Crikey, this is big place." It looked like there were about six hundred people in that night with a maximum capacity of around two thousand five hundred. They were playing an awful lot of pressing like stuff on the Jayboy label and I thought this is crap. The Meccas got the best rarities which to be fair it did at the time. I had not met Russ Winstanley before and I remember a bunch of lads from Nottingham giving him a really hard time because of the stuff he was playing. They were asking for records he simply didn't have at the time so they told him why doesn't he put on somebody who can. I happened to have got shoved to the front as Russ asked me who I was. "I'm Kev Roberts from Nottingham," I told him, and so he put me on, thanks to the helpful enthusiasm from my crowd. I went down well. I must have made the right impression because Russ asked me if I wanted to work at the Casino every week and of course I replied "Yeeaaahhhh!"

And so to 1974, and of course the buzz words were northern soul. I was only seventeen at the time and we were breaking new ground with sounds of our own: Lou Ragland's 'I Travel Alone', 'The Joker' and 'Strings A Go Go'. Then the commercial angle crept in and music industry people started turning up, writing articles about the Casino in *Blues and Soul* magazine. Television cameras began to appear for the first time and Pye records in particular began to latch on to what was happening, and they soon set up a division to start releasing stuff that would appeal to the new kind of audience. Unlike The Torch and The Twisted Wheel, two venues that only ever got bad publicity for the drug culture, the Casino was getting good, positive publicity, attracting growing numbers of people from far and wide. At its peak Wigan was pulling regular attendances of well over two thousand people and northern soul was a household name.

And what of my lost fortunes? After the Casino I decided to go to New York to see what I could find. Whilst I was there I met Lloyd Michels who had this demo track called 'The Flasher' which I brought back to England hoping to get a record deal with it. I approached 20th Century Records who had previously released 'Reaching For The Best' but they didn't know what to do with my discovery, so I went to a reggae label called Creole in London, who didn't like it but put me in touch with Denis Berger, who was the manager of Route Records, who picked up on it and made it a big hit. It was even used as the theme tune on Radio One's Newsbeat but I didn't make any money out of it because I was too young and naïve. It even featured on *Top Of The Pops* and I was invited down to London to watch the recording but I couldn't afford the train fare and was too busy talking northern and all I wanted to do was find more records.

One fortune gone and one to go. During the late 1970s I met up with a record buying customer of mine called Les McCucheon, from Weybridge in Surrey, who was also a businessman. A little older than me and he knew what was what. He became my partner, importing records and making things fit for the Casion Classics record label like 'I'm Gonna Share It With You' and 'Green Onions'. By 1979, when *Quadrophenia* came out, we were dabbling in all sorts of music. There was an outfit making records for us called The Nicky North Band who were friends of Les's. They had a stab at a jazz funk record called 'Steppin' of which we pressed a thousand copies and sold them to a store called The Record Shack, who then re-ordered it, by which time we needed a label so Record Shack became Shakatak and they went on to be signed by Polydor. I remember Les saying to me, as clear as day," Are you in or out?" as we only managed a five hundred quid advance between the lot of us. I thought there was more money in trying to find really rare records like 'Better Use Your Head' by Little Anthony And The Imperials than there was in the jazz funk game so somewhat short sightedly I let it go and I lost another fortune.

The rarity of the scene meant that small clubs that did play these records were very closely related in the beginning. The Twisted Wheel had a lot of credibility because it was playing really black records by singers like Bobby Bland but it was a certain deejay in a club in Wolverhampton called the Catacombs who everyone considered god-like because he discovered so many great records that were taken up to the Wheel, and his name was Carl Famer Dene. He found Richard Temple's 'That Beating Rhythm' on Mirwood Records and nobody believed that it existed because you had to go the Catacombs to hear it. He could find the records but he wasn't in a position to break them in the Catacombs because it closed at midnight. The Wheel, on the other hand, stayed open later and so became more prominent and able to break records to a bigger audience. As a deejay, your ability to break records was absolutely vital if you wanted to stay ahead of the game.

The difference betweenWigan Casino and the Highland Room was that Wigan had the fastest tempo of any all-nighter, and the tempo was absolutely critical because it was a massive ballroom full of two thousand kids, ninety-five percent of them on amphetamines. Some of the big lads must have figured out all the different ways into Wigan to check out the chemists that looked like they didn't have the greatest security. They used to drive down in crews from all over the country and whichever way they came you could bet your life there would be a chemist shop en route that would be broken into and whatever uppers they could steal they would.

The drugs utterly took hold of the dancers and came to dictate the tempo of the dancefloor. If a person is swallowing by midnight and speeding by three in the morning, then you'd best be ready with something dammed fast to play. It meant that there was no such thing as blowing your spot at the Casino. You can imagine the collective downer if two records on a row bombed out. The atmosphere would palpably slump and all of a sudden it would be a drag so the Casino was less adventurous in terms of breaking records than the Highland Room. It was not the environment to be playing nice sweet Philly sounds. The other peculiar thing was a lot of the records that took off had drug references in them. 'Blowing My Mind To Pieces', 'Cracking Up', 'Ten Miles High' - and then there was the Invitations' "gotta get my gear out ready for winter's near."

I mean to explain how crazy it would get. The legendary dancer Frankie from the Torch - everyone would get out of his way and he knew it. He was one of those guys who had a strong physique who could run up to the wall and do back flips off it. He'd do things with such astounding athleticism. I did notice in the Wigan period that you always

141

got the ones doing aeroplane spins. They twirl faster than the eye can see. In fact I saw a guy at Cleethorpes Pier locked into doing one when suddenly he came to a stand still, blood coming from his eyes, mouth and ears. He just blew up and it was upsetting because it was right in front of the deejay area too.

When I'd be going to these places they'd all be high as kites and those were the parts of the records they'd sing. In tandem with the drugs and how the tempo at different clubs happened, one of the other key things that defined northern soul was the gradual division of the crowds and their allegiances to the styles that were played by certain deejays. The main division came with the rivalry between Russ Winstanley and Ian Levine. As Russ grew in stature, the Casino developed its own crowd, which was very different to the Highland Room, so Ian Levine was king of his castle and Russ was king of his.

KEB DARGE - DEEJAY

My sister was a mod in the 60s and when she played me Motown records, I loved them. Then she got into all that hippy stuff and I didn't because I was only twelve or thirteen at the time and didn't want to hear folk whining on about the Vietnam War. Nowadays you've got all these escape routes like "I'm going to be a musician or an artist." "No, you're going to work in a factory and you're going to stay there for twenty years and you might get the key to the executive toilet" and that was your future. If this is it and I'm trapped, I'm going to escape for a wee while. The alternative scene was all about urban discos or you could go and bite the heads off chickens and piss in your jeans. Be a Hell's Angel or a hippy; but there was nothing about those scenes that was club orientated. My sister's escape was heroin and mine was trying to chase tunes across a dancefloor. Northern soul didn't exist in the real world unless you were in it.

DAVE EVISON – DEEJAY

My deejay-ing career began unexpectedly as a young squaddie serving in Northern Ireland between 1968 and 1972, when the sergeant major asked me to step in for the civvies who hadn't turned up for the do in the mess. Strange beginnings, but I began my northern soul career in Stafford at The Top of The World Club before going on to Wigan Casino, where I established myself as Mister Oldies, a label that stuck with me throughout my career. Back in the early Casino days things were so different. The scene was growing rapidly and it had gone like a roller coaster through The Torch and The Twisted Wheel and really had kicked off in a big way by the time it got to Wigan and became a national phenomenon.

From the one or two cars that had made the long distance journey to the Wheel to fleets of coaches from all parts of the country turning up at Wigan. The music policy hadn't changed up until then but the Casino Oldies scene changed all that and I must say that I can probably be blamed for the straw that broke the camel's back. The Oldies scene took away the whole notion of what the scene was about and as it grew and grew in popularity the audience began to divide, and today there is something sadly missing from the northern scene, and it probably started at the Casino, and that is respect.

When I used to go to The Torch and The Wheel, it always used to feel like it was a privilege to be there. It was like being back in the Army. You did what you were told, you listened to what the guys on the stage were playing as well as looking up to them. Not to say Martin Ellis because it was Martin Ellis but because he played great music and

143

you never knew what he was going to play next. And so after a lifetime of being a deejay, anyone who would like to pay me a compliment it would be to come up to me after my spot and say, "Hey Dave, man, that was great." And I haven't heard anything like that for years.

Don't get me wrong. I would have been happy to have stood behind a cardboard cut out, remaining the mystery deejay at Wigan. It wasn't an ego trip because I genuinely wanted to be thought of as one of the lads and to educate the youngsters on the scene and give them the opportunity that had been mine ten years earlier. Listening to different people and their musical tastes that I respected and to whom because of my respect for their knowledge I actually listened to them. I know this must sound corny but I feel this has always been an important aspect of the northern soul scene. There is no room for superstars. There are certain names I could mention that tried "the great I am" act but soon realised it didn't work. The people who gained respect were, I like to think, people like myself who danced to the music until it was time for their spot, did their spot and got back on the dancefloor. Admittedly it was hard to keep your feet on the ground when Wigan Casino was at its peak. It was huge, constantly on television and in the press and it was very easy to get carried away with your ego.

IAN DEWHURST - NORTHERN SOULER

Once we got sophisticated with travelling from venue to venue, we used to get down to Blackpool, the Highland Room, and spend three or four hours in there, then it'd be about a forty minute drive over to Wigan Casino. The great thing was that as you drew up, there was a tangible excitement in the air because you knew you were walking into a cauldron of energy and you had to have your membership ready to get in so it had that sense of

144

community as well. The entrance to the Casino was tatty and it was really busy; there would be steam coming out of the entrance. I've seen that happen in different cellar clubs before but for a building that big, as soon as you walked in the whole thing hit you. There's a really fast record playing, clouds of condensation hit you in the face and then you hear the synchronised clapping like thunder. When I'd go to places like Cleethorpes Pier, all you could hear was the "stomp stomp stomp" as if it was from the dancing. It was surreal. There's this ballroom jutting out to sea and all you can hear is the pounding of feet and the clapping of hands from over a mile away.

There was only one Golden Era of northern soul. I think we found all the great records between 1972 and 1976 and there was only one definitive playlist. Now you can argue as to how many records were on that list but it's no more than two hundred songs. The absolutely stonking dancefloor fillers like Tony Clark 'Landslide' and Gloria Jones 'Tainted Love'. Having said that, the ethos of the northern soul scene has continued. That exclusivity is still there. When the whole rave scene went ballistic in the late 1980s it felt like twenty years on. Lots of white working class people off their heads on uppers in basements dancing to fast music with this intense loving attitude. It's less so that rave culture is this generation's version of northern soul. More than that, northern soul was the UK's original rave culture and we can all be proud of that.

We were dealing with a depressed landscape. There wasn't a great deal there apart from steelworks and coal mines. You had people doing this boring repetitive hard work during the week. When they went out at the weekend to the working men's clubs, they really wanted to go out to the clubs until midnight and going out just wasn't going to be enough for them anymore. The first hint that I got that there there was anywhere for me was when I met some mods when I was around sixteen years old, in around 1971 to

145

1972. I probably had about a thousand to fifteen hundred records at the time and by the time I'd gone to a Motown night in a pub in Cleckheaton, I saw there blokes in blazers with the symbol of a torch sewn on the breast pocket. "What's that thing for mate?" I asked. "It's a soul club," one of them replied. "They have an all-nighter every Saturday."

"Well, I'm into that stuff too," I told him. He shook his head. "You won't know this stuff. This is northern soul mate."

It was even more underground than a movement. When I went to the Torch it felt like I'd entered a secret world. The mods that became the soul lads seemed to carry themselves better, with an air of superiority to the average beer-swilling factory guys. The lads had up to the minute fashions like mohair suits and the girls looked better than your average girls, well dressed, slinky and way ahead of the rest.

GARRY WHITE – NORTHERN SOULER

My first introduction to soul music was back in 1969 at my local youth club. Somebody brought in a few records to play, the first being 'Earthquake' by Al Tnt Braggs followed by 'I Dig Your Act' by The Ojays. From there on in I was hooked and by the time I was fifteen, I was attending our local rugby club's twice weekly soul sessions and the atmosphere was just fantastic. In those days it was either soul music, scooters, and yellow braided blazers, or Black Sabbath, leather jackets and motorbikes. There was no contest. Blackpool Mecca was soon beckoning. At this time I was playing football in and around the Blackpool area on Sundays so after the game I would go through to Preston to the record shop in the bus station as there always seemed to be something I wanted in there. Then it was back to Blackpool for a couple of hours, waiting for my mates to come through from Barrow, where we all lived. In those days the Mecca was a whole new world for us, with the legendary Ian Levine and Colin Curtis spinning the sounds.

Over the next year or so I started to venture further afield to the Top Rank in Hanley, the Va Va's in Bolton, Samantha's in Sheffield and then the night I will always remember, my first ever night in Wigan Casino. The club had already been open a couple of months and I'd heard loads of good reports about the place so I jumped on the train from Barrow, watching people jumping on the train in droves as a dozen or so portable cassette players clicked into action. The tunes and the faces of those people remain etched in my memory forever more, and as we arrived in Wigan somebody asked, "What are we going to do now for three hours?" The answer came back," The chippy and then the Beachcomber downstairs in the Casino basement" where people congregated, waiting for the doors to open.

At approximately one-thirty in the morning, we joined the queue and all the talk was about what records were played the week before and what would they be playing this week. Call me stupid but I wasn't quick enough to react to the crushing surge of people, my holdall went one way and me the other, taking me several minutes to reclaim my bag, and then it was up the stairs and through the doors, watching people already out on the floor dancing while others were looking for places to set up their camp for the night. This is brilliant, I thought, but by eight o'clock the following morning, as Jimmy Radcliffe's 'Long After Tonight Is All Over', I was knackered; but then it was down to the baths for an early morning swim and something to eat. The journey back to Barrow was another experience as we relived the night's action on the cassette players. Over the next few years I visited the Casino countless times although, for various other reasons, not as often as I wanted. Every trip had its own story to tell, like the night Tommy Hunt was on. My sister informing me that she had her vanity case stolen

147

with everything in it, keys, cash and train ticket. Have you ever tried smuggling somebody off a train while having your tickets being checked the same time? Believe me, it wasn't easy, but somehow we managed it. Now, years later, along with my lifelong mate Bob Reilly, we still have a successful soul scene up here in Barrow and the records I have at home, thinking that they were out of date, are now back filling the dancefloor once again. Keep The Faith.

IAIN McCARTNEY – AUTHOR, NORTHERN SOULER

Coming from a rural town in South West Scotland, my interest in soul music was totally self-inflicted. I had no other siblings to advise me or parents who showed any interest in music other than listening to the radio so how I even began to take an interest in music escapes me. When I was old enough I started attending local dances regularly, where the bands were predominantly from Manchester and Liverpool, so soul music was a huge part of their repertoire blasting out in the local youth club where I became a deejay, my only piece of equipment being one record player; so it was one record playing, take it off when it stopped and quickly replace it with another and so on and so on.

The youth club was actually a spin-off from a long established boys club and in the years before I joined, the organiser had taken a number of lads to Whitby for a camping holiday. When I became a member of the club, those holidays had switched destination to Blackpool and having visited the place before for the illuminations, I was up for ten days on the Riviera Lancashire. This, remember, was the late sixties, and the town was absolutely heaving during the long summer season.

The lads who went camping were quite a mixed bunch so a handful of us headed for the Pleasure Beach. As we headed towards the entrance, I spotted a bunch of girls heading in the same direction towards a building resembling the shape of a helter skelter so I decided to see where they were going. 'The Casino Sunday Dance Club' read the sign; and that was that. Everything else was put on hold as I paid in and walked through the door over to the staircase.

I had no idea what the music they were playing would be like but there were girls and we could drink underage so that was enough. Oh, and there were also a couple of go-go dancers, but they were soon ignored as the previously unheard magical sounds filled the air. Tunes I'd never heard before, danceable tracks that kickstarted a passionate love affair with the Casino that lasted a number of years, and a place that's still there today, conjuring up so many happy memories of those distant nights every time I pass the place even today.

Of those unknown tunes that the deejay Gary Wilde - a guy I got to know very well - played, there was one in particular that from the second I heard it it became my all time favourite tune, 'Little Darlin' by Marvin Gaye, and as soon as I arrived home, it was down to my local record shop to see if they stocked any of Marvin's albums with 'Little Darlin' on. As luck would have it, I did find one that kept me happy until I managed to buy the more expensive import copy of the single.

In later years I visited the famous Blackpool Highland Room but it wasn't what the Casino was. The music was different of course but the Casino will always remain closest to my heart, as will Blackpool. Those soul memories of the town don't simply hinge around those two nightspots. Other visions of the past from a soul perspective are conjured up whenever I return to Blackpool these days to spend a soul weekend either at the Tower Ballroom or Winter Gardens, where a record shop once stood on the corner not too far away from the world famous Winter Gardens ballroom. The shop sold loads of great soul singles and albums and it was the place where I managed to get a copy of 'Open The Door To Your Heart' by Darrell Banks and many more such great tunes. On Victoria Street, Gary Wilde had his little kiosk selling newspapers along with his secret stash of soul singles under the counter. I'm convinced that the many people strolling past, by the sizeable bunch of people clustered around his kiosk, wondered what the hell was going on, leaving me wondering if I ever brushed shoulders with the deejay Ian Levine or even Pete McKenna.

Another place sadly no longer there was a small amusement arcade just across the road from the Coral Island amusement complex. It had a jukebox like no other, full of Tamla Motown EPs, decorated in record sleeves, packed full of sounds that had us up and dancing. I recall somebody actually mentioning it on one of those Manchester-based soul shows. On Cookson Street there was the legendary Sinfonia Records, owned by the equally legendary Sandie, who knew everything there was to know about most music genres, who was mentioned numerous times in *Blues and Soul* magazine.

I discovered *Blues and Soul* around the same time as the Blackpool Casino, quite by accident, walking into a local newspaper shop to see a girl I knew who I used to go to school with. I grabbed a copy quickly, handing over the money as I dashed out of the shop with all thoughts as to the real reason I went into the shop in the first place forgotten. Soon after, I became a regular avid reader, as my record collection got bigger and bigger thanks to the Dave Godin column purely because if he said that a particular record was good then it was good.

At that time football was the love of my life with music being my bit on the side but one that I was never going to leave for the other. Old Trafford beckoned me from afar most weekends when I suddenly became aware of another Mancunian venue called The Twisted Wheel on Whitworth Street. I was an innocent abroad so to speak, so when I got approached in Victoria Station by two older guys in suits who asked me where I'd been, telling them I'd been to the Twisted Wheel, I was taken by surprise when they asked me if it was okay for them to look through my bag.

The Ritz Ballroom in Manchester was okay, admittedly not a soul music only venue but thanks to some free tickets on the door, it was the place to be before the Wheel opened its doors. Football reigned supreme and I soon found myself up and down the country taking in both home and away games when I started to hear about yet another Casino. This time it was in the town of Wigan and according to all the rumours, it was fast becoming the place to be, and only a short train journey from Manchester, but still I remained faithful to my first love. If I'd have had friends into the scene, I would certainly have found myself strolling down Station Road on my way to Wigan Casino to see for myself what it was all about; but it just wasn't to be.

I continued deejaying at the youth club although only a few people showed any interest in the music I was playing so I began helping out a lad who owned a mobile disco. Okay, I had to play the popular sounds of the day, but for the last hour of the night I was allowed to turn the place into a disco extravaganza. Time passed and I got married, meaning that the deejaying stopped but the football continued. One afternoon I bumped into a guy I knew simply to say hello. He was into the same music as me and lived nearby so we shared regular meetings, during which he gave me a pile of magazines along with some CD compilations and my world slowly began to change again.

Those magazines whetted my musical appetite so I took out a couple of subscriptions, eventually buying up back issues that I never knew existed that were going cheap on Ebay, in between listening to more and more of my old music I'd lost touch with over the years. Local soul nights were arranged and once again I found myself behind the decks, discovering that the old buzz was back bright and strong. I started going to soul nights in Carlisle as well as the

Blackpool soul weekenders. I also went to some live concerts where I met the likes of Edwin Starr, Duke Fakir, Martha Reeves, Ben E King and Brenda Holloway. Unexpected moments, meeting some of the great soul legends, that left me feeling far more excited than some of the footballers I'd brushed shoulders with.

At one of the regular venues I deejayed at, the manager was constantly asking me to put together a weekender so after listening to him several times I decided to do something about it. I contacted Kev Roberts at Gold Soul to ask if he would be interested in putting something together. Kev paid us a visit to check out the venue and so the Dumfries Northern Soul and Motown Weekender was born. A message on social media asked if anyone fancied doing a soul show leading to regular events, something I never imagined would happen in my wildest dreams.

Sadly the Covid virus brought things to an abrupt end as the studio became strictly out of bounds before it eventually moved away. Something else I would never have imagined myself receiving was a CD from a record company in the Bronx inviting me to play a couple of tracks of my choice from it. Something else I surprised myself with was writing a book associated with the music I loved. Prior to that I have written over two dozen books mainly about the football team I've supported through thick and thin over many years. I always wanted to do a book on my music scene, despite me not being as clued up as some are, but having amassed an awesome collection of fanzines and magazines, I decided to give it a go.

After contacting Howard Earnshaw from *Soul Up North*, he allowed me to put together regular features on my collection of magazines and fanzines that slowly inspired me to write the book, a history that was different to anything else. A publisher was contacted and after a lot of long nights and hard work *Soul In Print* hit the shelves. So that is my story, not as vivid or in depth as some out there but I'm more than content to have contributed to the longest lasting music scene in the world, having played the tunes to a receptive audience, and enjoyed a meal at the same table as Martha Reeves, as well as meeting and befriending many people for life. As Timi Yuro once sang, 'It'll Never Be Over For Me', or perhaps as Martha once sang - 'Come And Get These Memories.'

MATTY MORRIS – SKINHEAD, NORTHERN SOULER

In my younger days I remember days out with my family down the local working men's club, seeing my uncles and friends dressed in skinhead clothes dancing to Madness and Two Tone. My mum and dad were both ex-skins and my dad, going one further, became a mod. Northern soul and the scootering scene started back in the day between leaving school and starting college in 1992. Not long after getting my first scooter, which was a dream of mine for over one year after getting into the mod scene. For us, chart music was dead and our escape was old music. Not knowing the scene then as I do now, we loved the mixture of different sounds not to mention the dancing that had a style all of its own. We wanted to dance but it all looked so alien. It seemed familiar to soul and Motown yet different. I remember saying to my mates just dance and we'll be fine. We were all movers and somehow taking the piss or letting go, we were pulling it off. It felt good to let go and find a crowd of like-minded people.

With a passion for scooters and northern soul, I was already getting involved with the old vintage music from my childhood. Time progressed, going on rallies and enjoying many great memories. I got married, my wife fell pregnant and so we bought a house and gave birth to my daughter. The Camber Sands rally really kicked the scene from northern connoisseurs to open top blow you all away all-

153

night dancing. My passion to dance to what I called scooterist northern soul grew and grew, mixing with skins, punks, mods and indie types all under one roof. The Camber all-nighters seemed to take over me to the point where I wasn't doing the scootering side of things no longer. By now I was and had been a skinhead since 1996 but I found myself going from northern soul and reggae rooms. Clothes became baggier, hair longer and less macho, some would say. Maybe I was a part of creating the new look and passion with a small bunch of northern soul dancers, very like-minded people, springing from the bad old days of youths finding their feet, intolerant of other groups and gangs with different musical tastes.

The scootering scene had whipped us up into a frenzy and shown the best of all cults. Perhaps we were a generation younger and more tolerant that had enjoyed so many different musical passions that a new long lasting subculture was about to be born. Northern soul culminated this need within wanting to dance all night to something we loved and related to. Of the eighties and nineties, where everything seemed to be a remix of old, this was northern soul and for me the birth of the soul skin. Not a big group of people, they were on the fringes and you'd see them shuffling around, clearly influenced by northern soul with their roots firmly in reggae and the skinhead way of life, with a passion and love of soul music coupled with dancing and partying hard. Somehow those Camber moments made the soul skin for me. My life in the scooterist scene had been going for a while and I was an established shuffler but I left the competitions and bigger moves to the chosen few. I remember on one occasion when a friend struck up enough bravado to attempt some northern soul dancing. After the conversation he walked across the floor and started dancing only to realise it was in fact a change of record before the dance final. Thankfully it didn't deter him and he enjoyed plenty of shuffling about come the future.

My life was hitting the seven year itch and not my itch. A new outlet was needed thanks to Camber kicking off my passion for dancing. A new outlet was needed and although I was in a transition from scootering to northern soul, I started attending the breakaway scootering movement that had started to run dedicated soul do's in and around London, Essex and the South Coast. I was loving the music, hearing new, previously undiscovered sounds. However, instead of helping the situation, my wife and I were becoming more distant. Someone had caught my wife's eyes, and arguments and accusations soon followed, an admission that I was no longer loved giving vent to a feeling of despair from me. My marriage finally culminated in me finding out about the affair she was having with the person I initially suspected. My mindset was horrible and I poured myself into northern soul, trying to better myself. My dancing seemed to be stale, stagnant, unpolished and lazy, just like me and my wife. I video taped my dancing and said to myself," You need to sort yourself out son."

It was as if I was somehow trying to change myself through my dancing. Maybe a sad logic but we all deal with our problems in different ways. I started changing my shuffles, reflecting on past and present dancers I'd seen and known on the scene. I tried to reinvent the dance and somehow came up with a plan. Camber Sands and I'd be ready for everything it threw at me. Practising was easy whilst making dinner late in the house. Anytime was good. I was escaping and the music was working out to what you loved was easy. The time was fast approaching for the rally and there I was, Saturday night in the reggae and ska room. Time was fast approaching for the deal, talking with some fellow skinheads who were older than me and not into soul music. I was at a table drinking, as I had done most of the day. Somehow I've never been into drugs but I have been blessed with an ability to drink without affecting my dancing. The passion and the music take me over. Don't get me wrong, I sweat buckets and get tired, even knackered, but I carry on going. The competition was fast approaching as I told the lads at the table, "I'll be back in a moment," and I got up and walked across the dancefloor, asking a mate to look after my braces, wallet, keys and cash. My transition to soul skin wasn't complete that night but what the hell. My tonic trousers were a little tight but I had my Loake brogues on.

The records flowed as my ex entered the room arm in arm with a new affair, trying to be discreet but I knew what was going on. Life goes on, I said to myself but deep down I still wanted some payback, some revenge on her for the reason my life was no longer what it was along with my hard work, my laziness, my harshness, my nastiness. A good friend once told me to tell the fella who was with her never to show his face in front of me again and the guy heeded my words. My friend added that once you kick the shit out of him and wreck his car and his family, he can turn up whenever he wants. I had chosen a peaceful path, however tempted I was, because I always told myself that I would kill a man who robbed me of my family, my wife, my daughter. It was close that night as the words in my head rang out loud and clear:" You'll never win the competition." This was my passion, the competition, and soon the passion flowed, the tunes rang out loud and I danced. It has been noted by many that they see me smiling when I'm dancing and that's because I enjoy the music so much. I love it like a drug. People were getting tagged out but I was alive in my mind, body and soul, forgetting everything and everybody, that is until the numbers started to drop with the ex and her new boyfriend still in the room.

I had been knocked and banged earlier on Friday evening, almost goaded by two guys dancing and showing off but I kept a lid on it, only just. They looked on me with amazement, shaking hands and congratulating me after trying to impress my ex with their moves, now sorry for what they had done and they seemed genuine in their apology. People were amazed that my dancing had changed or was I just imagining that? After all the changes in my life I probably was as the old dancing splits came out, leg kick then down and up on a twist onto the other knee and back up spinning. Doing that move is always a painful affair, leaving bruises and pain, but I was having fun. The moves I'd learned in the working men's clubs, practising in the kitchen at every possible spare moment while cooking dinner and looking after my baby, paid off handsomely.

I was there in full flow as the new boyfriend left. What a shame but it inspired me and gave me confidence. I now know him and there are no ill feelings. It's just life and we always say hello to each other. I don't remember how many songs were played that night but the ultimate happened, the ex tagged out and I think that left five of us in the battle to win the competition. That was it, I got my revenge, strange and silly to look back on but the feelings were still with me. I was almost going to leave the dancefloor, feeling like my job had been done, that I didn't need to win it anymore when my mate said," Come on Matty, you're the only one here who can beat Will." They were kind words that inspired me, people looking like they were believing in the new me. The final kicked off with only three of us in contention. High kick drops and leg sweeps, luckily no split pants which I'd done a few times in the past. However, the fatigue was setting in with all three of us, each keeping an eye out on the other, hoping that nobody would have the strength to throw another big move into the equation, knowing I'd have to equal and better a move. The passion and free flowing dancing was oozing from me, sensing the fun side of things was disappearing into a challenge not only to win but to please the crowd as well.

The champ from the previous two years was still in with a shout with my fitness levels telling me I could win this. I heard the new song was coming to an end and I pulled off one special move at the end where I jump through my leg whilst holding my ankle with my hand. As Frank Wilson's 'Do I Love You' finished, it was a nervous wait, until I was awarded the third position; however, I had not realised that they were announcing the winner third, which was me. I was ecstatic at being the winner of the Camber Sands Northern Soul dancing competition. I think that was the culmination of the new me forced upon by the powers that be. I'd done it. People cheering and congratulating me as well as the other two guys in the competition. It's all part of it I guess, a personal challenge and the icing on the cake. Amid the celebrations I heard a pretty young girl asking my ex, "Who is that?" My ex replied, "He's my husband" to which I promptly turned and told her "Not anymore." After receiving the trophy, which was a gold coloured scooter, I walked back to the reggae room via the northern soul room surrounded by people shaking hands and backslapping me for my victory. I met and became friends with so many people that night and as things turned out, I was the third or fourth person to win the competition in nine years. Back in the reggae room I put the trophy down on the table, prompting one guy to ask where I had stolen that from. He and his mates simply didn't believe me until the deejay announced that the new northern soul dancing champion was sitting in the room after which loud applause sounded out, complete with more handshakes and hugs for a job done well, and I left Camber a better man than the one who entered earlier that day.

I returned home the next day and had a good chat with my daughter, who was five at the time, explaining to her that the trophy was very important and that she should treasure it. She was genuinely impressed although it was only a small scooter trophy but one I might not ever win again. It was my experience fighting a battle between good and evil trying at the same time to leave out her mum's actions. She would never understand how I related so much

158

to the music life and hardships. The story went along the lines of how I'd conquered my demons, my fears and won. An emotional man who channels his feelings constructively is a powerful person and far too many stories are about destructive behaviour. In fact the more I thought about it, mine was a story that could make a good child's book. She loved it and hopefully it taught her some of life's experiences but I was also telling her the truth when I said I may never win that trophy again because soul dancing comes from the heart and flows with a deep passion and determination. It should come from the heart and each song should mean some emotion that is personal to you and reflect your movements. I don't think that I will ever re-create the passion to dance as I did that night at Camber. I chose the peaceful route instead of violence and it showed in my dancing. In short I turned my life around that night. Matty The Chimp Morris.

IAN PALMER – NORTHERN SOULER, MUSICIAN

Where do you start when somebody asks you to put down in writing all your thoughts and feelings about the northern soul scene? After all, the scene is a bit like the 60s - if you can remember it then you weren't really there; but through the blur of it all, I laughingly call my memory, there are certain moments that seem to be as clear as day when they happened. I was too young to go to clubs like The Torch and The Twisted Wheel so my first real introduction to the scene was back in late 1974, when after travelling for what seemed like an eternity, followed by hours queueing in the freezing night air, I found myself for the first time walking on to the balcony of Wigan Casino. As if on cue, 'Leroy's Tears' blasted out of the speakers and the whole place went wild. I'd never seen a crowd that big react in such a way. People running downstairs to grab one of the few remaining spaces on the dancefloor. To this day, when I recall that special night decades ago, I can still remember the heat and the smell of the place. I was hooked.

That was over twenty years ago and after dabbling in various other music styles both as a punter and musician, I find that something keeps calling me back and here I am now visiting more all-nighters than I ever imagined I would. Probably because at the time, few lads could afford cars or train fares so the long journey north could only be made once or twice a month as and when spare cash permitted. Luckily for us we had the Yate all-nighters, which were far easier to get to and blessed with the craziest crowd of people in the country.

I can still remember hitch hiking to the Casino with Dave Thorley, who lived in the same small Gloucestershire town as I did and the man I really blame for getting me into the northern soul scene. It used to take practically all weekend, sometimes me not getting home until the early hours of Sunday and even Monday morning. I think that the nomadic, nocturnal aspect to the scene was half the appeal and I'm sure we all have similar memories of the great times we spent travelling to and from obscure far away places to get to the all-nighters, some of which may well have been crap but the journey more than made up for that. No other music scene has lasted as long as the northern soul scene and judging by the number of venues dotted across the country, it shows no signs whatever of dying out. So if you're reading this book about the northern soul scene simply out of curiosity, then do yourself a favour and check out a soul night for yourself. Better still, one of the bigger all-nighters where you will hear some of the most varied, exhilarating dance music ever recorded. And if you are one of those soul fans who has given it up for one reason or another, make sure you find your way back because you just may well be very surprised just how many of your old mates are still about.

HOWARD EARNSHAW – NORTHERN SOULER

My first taste of soul music was at the local discos of Huddersfield with names like The Starlight, Lord Jim's and The Hifi Discotheque, all names that will live in my memory forever more. That is where I was introduced to the heady sounds of Stax Atlantic and of course Tamla Motown. The whole mod thing really excited me at the time, the suits with the ridiculously deep centre vents and large flap pockets, Ben Sherman shirts and highly polished all leather brogue shoes with the one black driving glove and the girls with their immaculate hairstyles, short fringes and extra long side pieces, and being in with the in crowd, we automatically looked down on anybody who failed to fit in with us. We were untouchable.

It wasn't too long after that magic word "import" hit my ears and we all started travelling further afield to hear the music that we cared so much for and then making my first ever trip to the Twisted Wheel, remembered as much for the music as being rolled before I even reached the club and relieved of what money I had on me. Then after the Wheel it was on to clubs that will be familiar to all those who had an ounce of soul in their bodies: The Torch, The Pendulum, Samantha's, Hinckley, Clifton Hall, Blackpool Mecca and of course the one club that the whole world would come to know about, Wigan Casino Soul Club.

I remember my first ever visit. Initial thoughts were that this is the perfect all-night venue, the balcony was overlooking the swirling bodies on the dancefloor below, the smell and the sounds in that first year. There was no competition from any other venue. It was just the place to go and in amongst all that, I was married, divorced and married again, in the scene and out of the scene although you are never truly out of the scene and of course well into the whole thing all over again. So here I am, now older yes but still committed to that friendly, esoteric soul music thing that hooked me back in 1967 and continues to please and entertain me today. And what doesn't surprise me in the least is there are hundreds of others out there that are still experiencing the same buzz. Well, that's what soul music meant to me and still means to me. Keep On Keeping On.

JAY HALL – NORTHERN SOULER

I was born in March 1991, so compared to most people on the northern soul scene I was a relative newcomer and didn't really come across any northern soul until 2007. Sixteen years old but I can still remember every soul night I got to and the people I met and I can still remember the first time I heard the music properly. Young and arrogant, walking into my dad's house and I was like," What's all this music about?" My dad turned to me, a typical old school dad and said "This is northern soul son, the music I used to listen to when I was your age." After listening to it for a bit, I thought to myself: this music is not half bad. After that day at my dad's I found out that there was a scooter club that used to meet up at a pub at the end of the road.

They were having an end of season do, putting on a couple of bands and deejays playing Tamla Motown and soul music. I thought to myself, I'll get a ticket, seeing as everyone I knew was going. When I got there I was amazed that the music had its own dance style going with the music. After that night I decided to do some research on it so out came the laptop and google, trawling my way through thousands of results and I admit I didn't have a clue just how big the scene was. There was mention of Wigan Casino, the Twisted Wheel and the Blackpool Mecca. I thought to myself that this seems like a really great scene but by that time I was really involved with the scooter scene so I was only learning the mainstream northern soul tracks like 'Do I Love You' and the 'Snake'.

162

It wasn't until 2008 that I actually attended my first proper northern soul do and I still remember it clearly. It was the 16th of February and the deejay was Dave Evison. It was a great night but I just wished so much that I knew how to dance properly. On that night I kind of made the decision in my head that the only music for me from now on was to be northern soul. I got a few CDs and started listening to more and more music and now I have an iPhone full of northern. After that I discovered vinyl, so it was round to my old man's where I nicked all of his records from the eighties, then it was up to the attic to nick all of mum's Motown. As I mentioned earlier, I couldn't really dance so I thought to myself I have got to learn to dance, so reluctantly I asked my dad for his help in my quest to dance. He showed me all the moves, beginning with the basic side backward forward shuffle footwork. With what he showed me I went up to my bedroom and practised for hours to get my footwork to a reasonable standard. Then I watched lots of different videos of dancers on Youtube to get the different moves and techniques.

So I went off again, practising for hours on end, starting with the basic backdrop and side splits, progressing from there on in, suffering many bruised knees and bent fingers along the way but the pain was all worth it now I could dance reasonably well. The northern soul scene has done a lot for me over the past few years, helping me to get on the straight and narrow since I arrived on the scene and away from the life I was once living, hanging around the streets and local estates causing trouble, smoking drugs and thinking that I was untouchable, a hard man when in reality I was only a young boy acting the part. I have managed to find a whole new way of life and a whole new lot of people and when they say that northern soul is a way of life, they truly do mean it. It has offered me great opportunities with one of them being a dancer in a short film called *Young Souls* by Dean Chalkley but the biggest opportunity I got was to play a dancer in the full length feature film called *A Northern Soul* by film director Elaine Constantine, a dream project for her as she was born and raised in Manchester.

DAVE RIMMER – NORTHERN SOULER

How did I get into northern soul and what does it still mean to me? What a question; like, what is the meaning of life? Just what is it that still has the power to drag me out of the house every Saturday night to spend a couple of hours travelling to a venue to spend eight more hours in a dimly lit dancehall then to go through another two hours getting back home? The simple answer is I still don't know but what I do know is, it all started a long time ago, back in 1973.

In 1973 I was the typical pimply youth who was just learning about many things in life like sex and cigarettes, best bitter and the lure of the dancefloor in northern soul discos. I grew up just outside Warrington, a town which through The Carlton Club had a long history of playing black music. I was still at school then so what attracted me to soul music? The choice was made for you, you either liked soul music or you didn't and if you didn't then you liked long hair, leather jackets smelling of oil and motorbikes. In those days I much preferred the smell of Brut 33 so I became a soul fan.

It wasn't an overnight conversion though. I used to buy all sorts of records but it's just that I gradually realised that I was buying more soul records than any other music, influenced by the lunchtime disco that played a continuous diet of soul music. It was this and the fact that the discos were run by a good mate's older brother so we got in free and that really introduced me to soul music in a big way. The records I heard there I bought with my pocket money. I also began to hear tales of The Torch ballroom in Stoke On Trent that some of the older lads were going to. Eventually I

164

plucked up the courage to tell my parents I was staying over at a mate's house, allowing me to go to an all-nighter at the Va Va's in Bolton.

This was the period when you could go out any night of the week and find a pub, a youth club or a disco playing northern soul. The records were all new and exciting and because of the scene being so busy, a new sound could be broken in within a month, after which you'd probably be hearing it twice a week at least. So that was my introduction to the music; but what does it mean to me? Well, that period in my life holds so many memories, it has always been wonderful. As I mentioned before, the other discoveries were important. Sex was, but you never considered going out with a girl who wasn't into northern soul. Best bitter and hangover parties where neighbours called the police because we'd played 'Mister Bang Bang' fourteen times in a row at full volume. There were cigarettes and other substances, and throughout, the steady beat of soul music that provided a constant musical background.

So many memories and all catered for in and around a tatty run-down dancehall in Wigan, which became the focus of the whole week. I'm sure that other writers have said all there is to be said about the Casino so I'll not dwell on the place as much as the era. By 1978, I'd accepted a job in North Wales which involved me starting work at six in the morning on a Sunday so that was the last of the scene for me for a while. My own musical tastes matured and I concentrated on buying albums as opposed to singles, still outside the mainstream music Joe Public still knew about. That's something I have always had and will always retain, the feeling of being one of the elite, one of the in crowd, one of the few lucky ones to be let into the secret of what real music is all about. Snobbery? Yes of course; but why the hell not? We all know that the only type of music that really matters is soul music, don't we?

I moved to the midlands in 1981 with a large collection of albums and much less singles, got married, had children, bought a house and got on with my life and my career. The northern scene was dead, a distant part of my youth, albeit a large part that was now all just happy memories. How wrong I was. Unbeknown to me, when the Casino closed the scene just didn't die. It moved on to my home town of Warrington, Stafford, and London. It didn't die, it just went underground, as I kept seeing adverts for all-nighters in Wolverhampton so eventually, with the wife's permission, went to one in 1986. I remember walking in thinking that I wouldn't know anyone until Pedro from Wolverhampton came over, telling me that he recognised me from many a soul night. It was just like old times, the music was the same and I enjoyed myself so much that once again I was hooked.

So here I am, still doing the all-nighters and soul nights and in my own way, trying to put something back into the scene through the magazine I edit called *Soulful Kinda Music*. I realise that I still haven't answered the question 'what does northern soul mean to me' so here goes. For me it's a feeling, a lifestyle, a love of the music and friends from all over the country, the joy at hearing a record you love and the greater high of managing to buy a copy of that record. The atmosphere at an all-nighter, the anticipation of next weekend's all-nighter, the deejays and the venues. It all get in your blood and it never goes away.

Also, for me these days, it's the thirst for knowledge to know more about the people who made those magical records some twenty and even thirty years ago. I've once again taken the rose tinted shades view of course, ignoring the bad aspects of the scene; but why dwell on the down side when we have such a strong, vibrant, knowledgeable, alive scene? As an entity, it cannot be controlled by one person but it does have a persona all of its own and thanks to the continuing development of that persona, the change in the

166

venues, the records, the tempo, the continuous changing thread of young and old people will ensure that the northern soul scene will survive forever.

SIMON STEVENSON - NORTHERN SOULER

I grew up in Blackpool, born in 1966, so inevitably northern soul became a part of me and my friends from attending the local youth clubs, starting off at Saint Paul's on Whitegate Drive, the first place I heard Motown and northern soul. It wasn't the kind of music my parents entertained. My dad referred to it as jungle music when the jungle scene kicked off in the 1980s. I played him some northern and he had to agree that it had musical merit. We soon found our way to Saint Cuthbert's youth club, a nice hall with what I recall as being a good dancefloor. There I met some lads who were older than me and could do all the right moves. Front and box splits and Olympic circles but they couldn't spin. It was around this time when I was officially too young to get in so I borrowed my brother's birth certificate, who was two years older than me, allowing me entry into the Norbreck Castle and then the Highland Room in the Mecca complex, the place where I first realised that I was a good dancer because during the northern soul sets, there would be about thirty dancers surrounded by an appreciative audience allowing us the chance to really show off. One day I saw a lad they called China jump in the air and touch his toes, with me thinking I can do that better. Up I went, made contact with my toes and wallop, straight down into box splits. There were yelps of sympathetic pain but it was no problem for me. I just drew my legs back together in a vertical position and finished with a high kick. This became my party piece move. My mum wasn't impressed that every time I arrived home from dancing, I had blood all over my socks from skinning my ankles on the floor. Ah well!

Time moved on, beer and dope were discovered and northern soul gave way to Roy Harper and Hawkwind. I still had all my records buried in a wardrobe at my dad's house in Blackpool and always thought oh they are going to be money, never realising that a lot of them were cheap bootlegs. The clock on the wall spins like a soulboy on whizz to show the passage of years. We're now late 2007 and a guy at work had been listening to Mark Lamarr playing some music he introduced as northern soul. These tunes seemed to impress my colleague, who in a warped train of consciousness linked that since I was from up north therefore I must know about northern soul. I knew the 100 Club did the all-nighters but I had no idea how huge the scene had become. After a few days searching the internet I discovered that there was stuff all over the place, the next one being a Soul In The City do in a club in Watling Street behind Saint Paul's Cathedral. I went and tried to dance, a bit clumsy at first but by the end of the night my legs had remembered what to do and I was recreating the walk I did back then.

A brief but fabulous club for my renewed love was in the back room of the Castle pub on Tooting Broadway, after which I soon found myself going all over the place. Bidds, the King Hall in Stoke, the 100 Club, the fabulous Bisley Pavilion, the Twisted Wheel, Northampton weekender and loads more small do's all over the south as well as attending the Blackpool weekender and Whitby. Mentioning Blackpool reminds me of an occasion in the 1980s when me and my mates used to nick in the Tower when it was raining. One day I had my Sony Walkman with me, listening to some northern, so I stepped onto the dancefloor of the Tower Ballroom and danced to myself for a few enjoyable moments until one of the security guys chased me off. I'm very fortunate that I can listen to music while I'm working and have found a fabulous internet radio station provided by somebody called Dave from

Manchester. Thanks to him I've now played classic northern soul to many of my colleagues, some of who know what the music is all about. Of course not to forget to mention and thank all the really great, beautiful people I've met over the last few years. I'm crap at remembering names but you all seem to be able to remember when and where we first met. Cheers to the great friends I've made and to all those I'm yet to meet.

JANE HARRISON – NORTHERN SOUL GIRL

It was another oldies night at the Casino, a time when old faces turn up out of the blue and check out what they've been missing out on or haven't as the case may be. Early 1979 and someone had actually taken the trouble to bring a camera to record the moment. I remember the night well because we couldn't get a coach together anymore in Wolverhampton as the friendly neighbourhood squad had scared the coach companies off and with the demise of the longstanding freedom bus, we had no choice other than for it to run from out in the sticks. The problem was that we all had to make sure this coach never came off the motorway or ventured into Wolverhampton or it would never make it out again. Meeting the coach meant that we had to get to junction ten of the M6 motorway before meeting up in Willenhall nearer the junction. It was also decided that we all meet up in separate pubs as the paranoia had set in within our circle and many of our number had recently been either lifted or scared away, plus it would look really odd if we all took the same bus at once.

We were supposed to meet the coach at nine-thirty and it was late, strange looks a-plenty from the passing cars, asking themselves why would a bunch of thirty people be stood on a motorway junction in the dark night? Were we waiting for the Queen or was it some mass hitchhiking exercise? When it pulls up there are as many people jumping out of the coach as those trying to get on, old friends, long time no see friends who I still know today. It's mayhem on the coach, caused by a combination of excitement and anticipation looking forward to a great night or we just happen to bring this behaviour out when we meet up with each other. It's a bit of both, spiced up with a bit of added chemical content.

First service stop Hilton Park; hang on as we've only just got on and this is still too near town so some of our number got off the coach and hid in the shadows until we set off again. Shortly afterwards we were off again and no more service station stops until we get to Knutsford, about to hit Junction 25 and we're nearly there, navigating our way through Wigan and on to Station Road bang on midnight. I'm off into the throng, needing to see someone who, unknown at the time, it would be the last time I saw for a year as he was due to be modelling her Majesty's latest work wear. I soon bumped into people I hadn't seen in ages while the last time I saw my mate Andy, he was being led away by some coppers after jumping the train to Wigan on a platform ticket and as a result was forced to move back home to Lancashire.

Little was I to know that some eighteen months later, I would rekindle my friendship with him outside Boots chemist in Blackburn and a friendship that saw us be best men at our weddings. Back to the night and it was a typical oldies night, full, hot and loud. I loved the oldies as the music gave me a reminder of why I fell under the intoxicating smell of black America. The night seemed to whizz by in more ways than one and before we knew it, we are out in the sunlight, eyes squinting in the cold early daylight. The mood in the coach is subdued with most people just wanting to get home for some peace and shut eye but not us, if we get back at the usual time, as it means there is only one hour before the pubs are open.

170

Some of us decide that Sandbach services was the best place to stop and for two pence you got a shower complete with towel. The coach dropped us back from where we set off from but some of us decided that the Vic was the best option. We don't have long to wait for the bus, it's Saturday morning and the bus is full of shoppers totally uninterested in our bedraggled bunch climbing up the stairs to the top deck. The bus pulls in and stops as everyone piles off and that's when the camera comes out, no smiles, no hugging, all of us just standing there. Some of the crowd in that cherished photograph are sadly no longer with us while others have attended each other's birthdays, weddings and so on. Another night," I've got us a lift, Jane, with the Clitheroe lot," Jill told me, and my heart sank after watching them downing pints of Guinness and lagers with a few smarties so I was hardly looking forward to the journey home. Our lift was a van, an old post van, and the company was excitable to say the least, hearing the words I did not want to hear as the contents of a friend's stomach spilled out all over the floor. "Thanks for the lift, lads, and see you in there."

So there I was, sitting there hoping for a bit of peace and not to be noticed, after all no leather, only my bright red coat, two jumpers and a scarf and hat. Then I heard this voice:" Sit with us sweetheart. Come up here and see what pops up." Oh yeah, the cheeky boys, the lads from Manchester. Oh change the record, I thought, sitting there asking myself if it was worth it going to Wigan. Off the bus and I was met by six punks shouting "Fucking soul shit." Oh not heard that before, but how could I run in these boots? How could they tell I was off to the Casino? I tried to ignore them but it got the better of me so I shouted back with all I had. "Just because you look different and like different music. I don't understand your taste in style or music. After all if you don't want to fuck me is a classic, then the electric chair will do it grand." That night I can't remember running as I eventually ran into my mates and had one of the best nights in Mister M's ever. They even played all the tunes I loved dancing to.

WILL VINCENT HUNT – SKINHEAD, NORTHERN SOULER

There's been plenty spoken and written about the history of the British soul scene, so despite decades of personal research, I won't try and recap with my own inaccuracies with who did what, where and when. This is purely a few snippets of my own experiences as I tried to personally recreate how it was in the early 1970s in amongst an ever changing scene. I've been a skinhead since about Easter 1982, some years after the originals, but being born in 70s Sunderland gave me little choice. From musical beginnings in ska and reggae, given a small helping hand by me and my brother Bob pinching Mam's collection of Blue Beat and Island, apart from a catchy collection of Motown and Stax tunes, I hadn't shown a lot of interest in soul music until I started attending mod clubs in Newcastle. This was a relatively underground scene, mostly full of teenagers, but many with a passion for tailor made suits, scooters and original 1960s gems, mixed in with a backdrop of soul, RnB, Motown and ska in a slightly cider fuelled haze.

There was a great buzz queuing up outside of mod all-nighters, slyly checking out the details on each other's clothing, eager to get on the dancefloor. I'd saved up my pocket money and dinner money to spend as much as I could afford on clothes and nights out. We'd scour second hand shops for original items and get the local tailor to do the alteration work on old two tone suits, sitting for hours sewing on cuff buttons and turning up trousers. I bought a pair of leather soled wingtip brogues from a shop in Hendon which were a pale imitation of the Cordovan lovelies I have

172

now but I thought they looked the business at the time. If you shopped around Newcastle you could still get basket weave loafers, buckle riders and Hawkins Moon Hop eleven hole boots and the charity shops were overflowing with Jaytex shirts and sheepskins for ten bob. I no longer fit into a size fourteen neckline but I still wear most of the shoes I bought back then.

We'd often head off for a weekend crammed into one of the older lads' cars, off to some grim town in Yorkshire or Lancashire for a pure soul all-nighter. I will never forget six of us squeezed into a beat up Ford Fiesta with non-stop soul music from the cassette player, destination the Twisted Wheel in Manchester. It was the club's monthly night off from Rocky's Queer club held there, which was a slightly disturbing fact for a naïve fifteen-year-old lad to take in. The venue had changed little since its hallowed days in the late 1960s, no massive dancefloor like many clubs had at the time but there were a number of smaller rooms in a dingy basement which wasn't a pretty sight. But the atmosphere, that was intense, and as the night went on, the sweat rained down on us from the low ceiling. My only regret from the night was getting ready at home thinking that a good choice of footwear for the night would be my new Riders, into which I'd previously hammered home around forty segs into each sole. A shiny wooden floor soaked in beer, talc and sweat didn't agree with a full set of Blakey's if you wanted to risk something more than a Harlem Shuffle.

I'd often head off to Keale with a good mate, Little Micky, my all-nighter bag slung over my shoulder containing a small towel and a bottle of Brut 33, before he acquired our own transport. We walked miles to the station, then a coach to Manchester, a bus to Stoke and another bus to Keale, feeling like we'd done a full day's travel. After a quick change in the toilets, we endured what seemed like marathon dance sessions before scabbing a lift back to Stoke and spending hours on buses long after the excitement had worn off. Always came back for more though, as the music, the friends and the atmosphere made it all worthwhile.

SPINS! There's always been a manoeuvre on the dancefloor that you can do or cannot do. The first became apparent at our regular Tuesday night spot called The Wreck, watching two old boys going head to head in a spin off competition dancing to Junior Walker's classic soul track 'Tune Up'. Always a trier, I've been spinning for years, mostly unsuccessfully. For me there's that moment when you carry off what seems like a perfect spin and an air of smug satisfaction washes over you, leaving you grinning until the end of the record. Then there are the other ninety percent of times when you spin like a top across the floor banging into people along the way, thanking your lucky stars that northern soul dancing etiquette allows you such misdemeanours without a fight breaking out as it would in other nightclubs. My worst ever spin of all time took place in the Soul Room on the Isle of Wight some years back when I went into a massive spin through what felt like a black hole in space and time. I landed up flat on my back and all I saw was nothing. Everyone had gone, the thumping beat had disappeared and I was staring up at a dark ceiling, totally confused, feeling like I'd been asleep for ages. Then a big door swung open and a bouncer appeared, holding out his hand, frowning at me with disdain. Apparently I'd spun across the floor and through some double doors into another room, so by the time I landed the doors had swung closed, shutting out any evidence of where I was supposed to be. As such I am genuinely jealous and in awe of all those of you out on the floor spinning effortlessly for what seems like an eternity. Consider my cap well and truly doffed.

OXFORD BAGS! Clothes have always been a big part of being a skinhead for me, a re-creation of all the original styles with an attention to detail and authenticity. From the work boots, rolled up Levis and braces, check Bennies, tonics, Crombies and beyond that all came out of the 1960s. I've always been what can only be described as obsessed in re-creating my own authentic image. As trousers started to get wider in 1971-1972, straight leg Levi Sta Prest evolved into parallels, waistbands and Oxford Bags. A million variations on the theme came and went but the bags were commonplace in soul clubs in the north like the Catacombs and the Golden Torch and later on Wigan Casino. I've had my fair share of parallels over the years with variations on the detail – waistbands, multiple pockets, crown flaps, leg pockets, buttons galore and made with enough material to sail a ship. In the true spirit of youthful one-upmanship the saying "biggest was best" often prevailed as it did with the biggest sideboards, most ticket pockets and button cuffs and mirrors on your scooter. I was at a scooter rally late one night arguing the point with my best mate Dosser about who had the biggest pair of Oxford Bags. I had some eighteen pockets, high waisted and thirty-two inch wide bought in Aflecks Palace on my way to Keale. So we agreed that when we met up the next time we'd settle the score once and for all. I heard through the grapevine that Dosser took the bet seriously enough to order a pair of thirty-six inch parallels knocked up especially for the bet.

With no time to see a tailor myself, as well as not wanting to be outdone, what choice did I have? Off to the fabric shop it was, where I bought some supplies, having never made a pair of trousers before in my life. It was a little daunting to say the least so I asked the advice of the shopkeeper. "I'm making a pair of trousers and I need some help," I told her, as we went through some leg measurements. "No problem," she assured me, as I told her: "They'll be quite wide, about forty inches, and I want plenty of buttons on them, say seventy-two or maybe eighty for good measure and there'll be a few pockets on them as well." The woman never raised a smile during the whole process, so with my mother's sewing machine I settled down to work armed with a piece of tailor's chalk and some optimism. My first attempt of a waistband and fly wasn't too successful but after a rethink and what must have been every night for two weeks beavering away like Rumpelstiltskin they were done ready for the Bridlington scooter rally, in 1989 I think. It was one of those moments when I walked into a very crowded pub, the place suddenly going deadly silent with everyone staring at my bags in horror and amusement. Dosser turned up in his crafted strides but they were no match for my home made bags boasting a sixteen-inch waistband, twenty-two pockets, seventy-two buttons and forty-two inch parallel legs that were enough to win any prize going for the biggest best bags; but since then I've learned that there's a trick to getting downstairs in them without falling down and how to piss in the gents without filling up my turn ups.

When I'm on about bags, I found an old seventies tailored pair with about forty-eight flaps, too many buttons and a good forty inch straight leg. I took them away with me to a soul week in the Canaries. First night on, I noticed that the zip catch was bust and wouldn't stay up so I carefully safety pinned them from the inside on with my safety pin then it was off to the do. My first trip to the toilet meant fiddling around with my safety pin for ten minutes, a rigmarole I knew couldn't continue. Next time in the bogs I realised that the trousers were so baggy I could roll up the leg, allowing me to piss out of one side, and this did get me a few funny looks later on in the night when there were no spare cubicles affording me a bit of privacy.

It will be a sad shame when the original crowd finally hang up their original leather shoes and the scene disappears for good. That said, there are a few youngsters doing the rounds, which is refreshing to see, not just nightclub tourists but genuine soul fans, some of them leaving me green with envy as they handstand and fly around with the exuberance of youth firmly on their side, but the core in my time has always been the old crowd who were there in the Casino and before and beyond. Hopefully by the time it disappears I'll be too old to backdrop – is there such an age? – and will have banked enough memories to bow out gracefully. After twenty-odd years going to nighters and dos, I've met a lot of good friends, chewed a lot of Wrigleys, ruined several pairs of shoes, leaving me trying to dance on an insole and a few nails, talked a lot of rubbish, split a few pairs of trousers, showed off a bit and been showed up, danced in the aisles to Junior Walker wandering around blowing his sax among the appreciative crowd, suffered various minor injuries, grabbed a couple of hours' kip after a long night dancing before riding my Lambretta home bleary-eyed and dehydrated and I've danced to records that made my hair tingle as well as making me laugh and cry. But for now I'm still dressing like it's forty years ago, still riding Lambrettas, and still making the most of the thriving scene that eases the opportunity to never ever grow up. All in all I'm pleased and proud to have played my part in what has to be the coolest underground scene in existence. Long may it continue.

BY THE SAME AUTHOR

NIGHTSHIFT

JOHN KING - AUTHOR OF *THE FOOTBALL FACTORY, HEADHUNTERS, ENGLAND AWAY, HUMAN PUNK, WHITE TRASH* AND OTHERS "Pete Mckenna's *Nightshift* gives a first-hand account into the legendary Wigan Casino. A heartfelt look at the music, the style and the drugs. This is another book written from the inside rather than the outside looking in."

JON SAVAGE - AUTHOR OF *ENGLAND'S DREAMING – A PUNK ANTHOLOGY*" *Nightshift* is a readable honest account of a Wigan Casino adolescence, the first of any substance that I've read. Pete doesn't play elitist games but writes with candour about the scene's saturation and of course its sheer joy. As a memoir of what it's like to be young, restless and weird across the north west, it is near unbeatable."

SHARON DAVIES – AUTHOR "Pete's colourful proses make the whole magical era real today with its powerful influence. No holds are barred here hence some readers might find his language a bit too realistic. This true story is wonderful fascinating reading warts and all."

ALEX PETRIDIS – AUTHOR "*Nightshift* is a fascinating insight into British dance culture in the 1970s. Immensely readable and written with the same breathless pace as, say, The O'Jays Working On Your Case."

SHERYL GARRATT – AUTHOR OF *ADVENTURES IN WONDERLAND*" Nightshift is a great read, by far the best thing I've read on the northern soul scene. It was really important to me that British kids who think it all started in 1988 understand that we have a history of hedonism that goes way back before that."

RECORD COLLECTOR MAGAZINE " –*Nightshift* is effectively the only first hand account of any substance written on the all night soul circuit of the 1970s. McKenna's recollections make for fascinating reading, a truly fascinating insight into one of Britain's most enduring music cults."

SOUL GALORE MAGAZINE " –*Nightshift* is not a pretty book. You would not want to encounter some of the characters who feature in this story but you can not deny the lifeblood that pulses through its covers. In one way or another we're probably all in this book somewhere."

WHO THE HELL'S FRANK WILSON

JOHN KING – AUTHOR OF *FOOTBALL FACTORY, HEADHUNTERS, ENGLAND AWAY, HUMAN PUNK, WHITE TRASH* AND OTHERS" I got into Petes's story very quickly and it works well, chugging along at a good pace. The whole idea of basing the plot around a rare soul record ties in well with the nature of the northern soul scene with a sad ending highlighting the loss when someone who is into a scene so strongly representative of their youth. It is a powerful book I can easily imagine as a good film. LOCK STOCK AND NORTHERN SOUL."

PAOLO HEWITT – AUTHOR AND JOURNALIST "Pete's story is really pacey and exciting so my question is who the hell's Pete McKenna and more importantly should you read his book? Answer as the man once sang: Indeed You Should."

MARK SERGEANT – MUSIC EDITOR SCOOTERING MAGAZINE "The book sums up the essence of the 'golden era' incorporating the seven esses. Sounds, substances, scooters, skinheads, sex and seven inch vinyl soul gems. A fictional journey back to the era of the world's first superclub. A sizzling scintillating story."

PETE HAIGH – DJ MAGAZINE WRITER "Pete's second opus is a mix of fact and fiction about 1970s life on

179

the northern soul scene in and around Blackpool and Wigan Casino. Hard times in which people are living a northern lifestyle with characters akin to those in Paul Abbot's gritty television series *Shameless* with a nod to Richard Allen's grubby skinhead series of books with a twist of *Quadrophenia* type chip on the shoulder. Pete lets you live the life whether you want to live it again or just enjoy the ride. Only you can say but I wonder what Frank would say."

Milton Keynes UK
Ingram Content Group UK Ltd.
UKHW021930281024
450365UK00017B/1018

9 781915 975089